Helion & Company Limited
Unit 8 Amherst Business Centre
Budbrooke Road
Warwick
CV34 5WE
England
Tel. 01926 499 619
Email: info@helion.co.uk
Website: www.helion.co.uk
Twitter: @helionbooks
Visit our blog http://blog.helion.co.uk/

Text © Gerry Doyle and Blake Herzinger
    2022
Photographs © as individually credited
Colour profiles © David Bocquelet, Tom
    Cooper and Ivan Zajac 2022
Diagrams and Maps: George Anderson
    © Helion & Company 2022 and Tom
    Cooper 2022

Designed and typeset by Farr out
    Publications, Wokingham, Berkshire
Cover design by Paul Hewitt, Battlefield
    Design (www.battlefield-design.co.uk)

ISBN 978-1-915070-64-7

British Library Cataloguing-in-Publication
    Data
A catalogue record for this book is available
    from the British Library

We always welcome receiving book
proposals from prospective authors.

CONTENTS

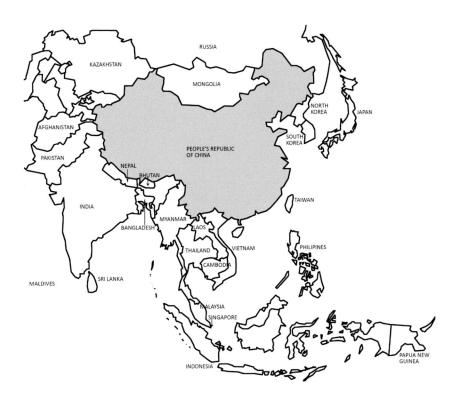

Note: In order to simplify the use of this book, all names, locations and geographic
designations are as provided in *The Times World Atlas*, or other traditionally accepted
major sources of reference, as of the time of described events.

ABBREVIATIONS

A2AD	Anti-Access/Area Denial		**LAC**	Line of Actual Control
AMRAAM	Advanced Medium-Range Air-to-Air Missile		**MRBM**	Medium Range Ballistic Missile
ASBM	Anti-Ship Ballistic Missile		**NATO**	North Atlantic Treaty Organization
AWACS	Airborne Warning and Control System		**ODIN**	Optical Dazzling Interdictor, Navy
C-RAM	Counter-rocket, -artillery and -mortar		**OTH**	Over-the-Horizon
CCP	Chinese Communist Party		**PLA**	People's Liberation Army
CEP	Circular Error Probable		**PLAAF**	People's Liberation Army Air Force
CGI	Computer-generated Imagery		**PLAN**	People's Liberation Army Navy
CIWS	Close-In Weapon System		**PLARF**	People's Liberation Army Rocket Force
CSG	Carrier Strike Group		**PRC**	People's Republic of China
ICBM	Intercontinental Ballistic Missile		**RV**	Re-entry Vehicle
INF	Intermediate and Short-Range Nuclear Forces		**SIGINT**	Signals Intelligence
IRBM	Intermediate-Range Ballistic Missile		**SINKEX**	Sink-at-Sea Live Fire Training Exercise
IRGC	Islamic Revolutionary Guard Corps		**TEL**	Transporter-Erector Launcher
ISR	Intelligence, Surveillance and Reconnaissance		**THAAD**	Terminal High Altitude Area Defense
ISTAR	Intelligence, Surveillance, Target Acquisition and Reconnaissance		**USSR**	Union of Soviet Socialist Republics
JDAM	Joint Direct Attack Munition			

ACKNOWLEDGEMENTS

Gerry

This book is dedicated to all the teachers who told me I'd amount to something. To all the people (mainly my incredible wife, Kara) who lived in the buildings that I was writing in, who didn't call the book police on me when I was just trying to make some money to feed my family. Thanks also to Juan and Chris, for helpful and kind feedback along the way, to all the smart folks who agreed to let me interview them, and to Blake for putting up with my editor/bully tendencies.

Blake

To my son, Henry, for filling the house with joyful toddler sounds and periodically kicking in my study door to visit me while I labored at this coalface. And to my darling wife, Ali, a real TC that kept the trains running on time while I "wrote about missiles or whatever with Gerry." Finally, a big thanks to my friend Gerry for bringing me in on this project (and to Kara for defending me against his bullying tendencies).

INTRODUCTION

China's DF-21D owes its inspiration to a visit from the US Navy.

In March 1996, USS *Independence* and USS *Nimitz*, nuclear-powered supercarriers, sailed through the waters surrounding Taiwan accompanied by two full battle groups. Together, the ships bristled with firepower: F-18s that could sortie dozens of times a day, each with nearly 14,000 pounds of ordnance; F-14s with AIM-54 missiles capable of wiping bandits from the sky hundreds of miles away; cruisers and destroyers with RIM-67B missiles to knock down incoming threats and BGM-109 Tomahawks to crush land targets. More than enough to punch a smoking hole through China's mainland defences.

The carriers and their escorts were there to make a point. In previous months, China had tested Dong Feng-15 nuclear-capable short-range ballistic missiles in these waters; practiced an amphibious assault; and held live-fire exercises, all within shouting distance of Taiwan's islands.[1] The tests and drills were backed with an assault of rhetoric, warning the Taiwanese that if they elected Lee Teng-Hui as president, China would consider it an act of rebellion and respond with force. The United States sought to communicate,

in no uncertain terms, that American naval strike capabilities could snuff out any misguided foray across the strait. American strategic dominance was on full display in support of Taiwan's continued independence.

At the time, China's coastal defences were built around Soviet-era systems such as the HY-1 and H-2 Silkworm anti-ship missiles, which were subsonic and could barely fly 50 miles. Their aircraft inventory was also rickety. Although the People's Liberation Army Air Force had acquired a handful of Su-27 fourth-generation multirole aircraft from Russia in the early 1990s, the bulk of its squadrons were J-7s – an indigenous version of the MiG-21 – and J-8s, a 1960s-vintage interceptor. Only the Flankers posed a threat to the US fleet, and there were so few that none were likely to get through the umbrella of missiles and air patrols surrounding an aircraft carrier. The People's Liberation Army Navy was only beginning to emerge from its origins as a so-called brown-water navy, oriented toward shore defence, and was no match for the combined might of two American carrier battle groups.

The American ships sailed through without incident, and their message was delivered: China could not stop a great power from operating nearby, even when the stakes were high.

For China, what it perceived as shameful impotence became a turning point.

Unable to modernize its bloated, outdated force quickly, China turned to technologies now referred to as *shashoujian,* or assassin's mace, to counter American military power asymmetrically. The shift spurred by the Third Taiwan Strait Crisis, as the 1996 confrontation came to be known, is most evident in its ballistic missiles. Its conventional arsenal mushroomed from a few hundred missiles to nearly 2,000 as it sought ways to hold its adversaries' forces at risk even if it could not match them gun-for-gun in the field. And to prevent a repeat of the embarrassing events of 1996, the People's Liberation Army wanted a new weapon specifically designed to keep America's navy at arm's length. A carrier killer.

Building on its successful DF-21 conventional ballistic missile, researchers added a warhead that could manoeuvre in its terminal phase – after re-entering the atmosphere – and hit a moving target. The resulting variant, the DF-21D, emerged into daylight in 2009. According to Western intelligence agencies at the time, it had not been tested against the sort of target it was meant to attack. But the Chinese military made it clear they believed it could destroy aircraft carriers and other surface ships at ranges exceeding 900 miles – well beyond China's home field and deep into international waters around the Asia-Pacific region.

For the next 10 years, the DF-21D inventory grew, and China became more explicit about what the weapon could do. Satellite photos showed tests against carrier-sized targets laid out in China's western deserts.[2] The missiles appeared in National Day parades, rolling through the streets on camouflaged launchers, the centerpiece of an ascendant nation's conventional deterrence.[3]

Amid the complex, long-term dance of threats and innuendo, the missile itself has only once been tested against a moving target at sea – an exercise in 2020 from which no concrete evidence of success emerged.[4] Even after that test, more than a decade after the missile first appeared, its most important capabilities remain a mystery. China's arsenal of DF-21Ds, some based deep in the mainland, represent an unproven, but potentially devastating, barrier to any power hoping to sail an attack force close to its shores.

The US military has taken notice. Although warships – including carriers – still routinely pass through the Taiwan Strait, the operating assumption is that anti-ship ballistic missiles would make a close approach to China during a shooting war costly and difficult. Whether the DF-21D works as advertised or not, it weighs on the minds of Western strike planners, affecting the trajectory of operations and spending priorities.

Absent a full-scale conflict, neither the People's Liberation Army Rocket Forces nor their Western adversaries can say whether the DF-21D would neutralize or destroy a carrier. China will not use the missiles outside that type of scenario, as 'real deal' launches would not only provide useful information about how the system works, but also demonstrate its weaknesses. The missile is a hole card in a billion-dollar poker game.

But information leaks out, intelligence agencies pry for details where they can, and previous research and open-source data provides hints of how the DF-21D works and how it might be stopped.

Indeed, the idea of an anti-ship ballistic missile is not new. Both the Soviet Union and the United States experimented with the concept in the 1960s, when almost any military system was seen as worth a try. The Soviets developed such a weapon, the submarine-launched, nuclear-tipped R-27K, but never fielded it because it counted against treaty limits, and because finding an aircraft carrier to begin with proved a towering barrier to success.[5] Nor are manoeuvring warheads new; the MGM-31B Pershing II used an internal radar to guide its re-entry vehicle to the target in the final stages of an attack.[6]

The precision needed for a ballistic missile to hit a ship at sea, especially if it is trying to evade, is staggering. The Pershing II had a circular error probable against a known, stationary target of 100 feet – about the width of an aircraft carrier at the waterline. The Pershing family, like the R-27K, addressed accuracy issues by using a nuclear warhead. Perhaps more important, both the United States and Soviet Union developed cheap, high-speed anti-ship missiles that could be launched from the surface, submarines, or from the air, providing more than enough punch to attack what was already an improbable naval threat to their homelands.

Even now, neither the US nor Russia has invested in developing modern anti-ship ballistic missiles, perhaps because both enjoy an advantage in geography and have huge fleets of quiet attack submarines, a proven force that can strike from below with even less warning than a missile screaming in from space. India and Iran, which also have an interest in keeping enemy ships far from shore, have tested anti-ship ballistic missiles with ranges of a few hundred miles, but have never struck a moving target at sea.

Even with present-day technology, the issue of how to make an anti-ship ballistic missile work well remains a formidable challenge. Finding the target is only the first step, and it is a colossal one. In millions of square miles of ocean, even a 100,000-ton carrier takes up almost no space at all, and the farther from the launch site it is, the farther it will move while the attacking warhead makes its malicious journey. Orbital sensors are the easiest solution to this problem, and since 2011, China has launched more than four dozen satellites with the declared purpose of reconnaissance. Many other satellites with less sinister official payloads may be useful for this mission during war as well.

Once there is a general fix on the target, the DF-21D can be launched, aimed at a swath of ocean. Satellites and other sensors may provide updates that narrow that swath. As the warhead heats up during its descent, it becomes shrouded in plasma, cutting off communications. Onboard sensors begin searching for a ship to hit, generating data that steer the warhead as it blazes through the atmosphere.

None of these steps – finding the target, transmitting guidance data to the missile, and using onboard systems to steer the warhead to moving target just a few hundred feet across – is easy, especially at the speed of a ballistic missile.

And attacking a defended target is even more difficult. The US has invested billions of dollars in upgrading its Standard Missile arsenal, particularly the RIM-161 SM-3 and SM-6 variants, which are designed to shoot down short- and medium-range ballistic missiles, and even satellites.[7] American supercarriers travel with at least three cruiser or destroyer escorts loaded with such munitions, and in the event of a ballistic missile attack, they would be able to engage each inbound target with several missiles. Lasers cannot destroy warheads designed to withstand the temperatures of re-entry, but may be able to blind their optical sensors, and other nascent technologies such as railguns may someday offer additional promise as a cheap way to shoot enemy missiles out of the sky.

The carriers themselves have their own countermeasures, including radar-confusing devices such as chaff clouds, floating reflectors and MK-53 Nulka decoys, which hover in the air behind a ship broadcasting signals to confuse and attract incoming missiles.

Of course, the preferred method of avoiding a DF-21D strike – or an attack by any ballistic missile system – is to keep it on the ground. So-called 'left of launch' measures can include cyberattacks, digital sabotage, jamming and airstrikes. The United States also has a constellation of staring satellites, Space-Based Infrared Sensors, to spot missile launches.[8] A ballistic missile attack on a US carrier strike group would be reported almost as soon as it leaves the ground, giving the fleet time to prepare its defences.

The idea of an anti-ship ballistic missile has taken root in China's military planning. The country is not only building more DF-21Ds but has developed an ASBM warhead for another such missile, the more numerous DF-26, billed as having a 2,500-mile range – more than enough to hit Guam from several hundred miles inland in China. In theory, that puts any naval adversary at risk long before it is in Chinese waters, let alone striking distance.

The latest Chinese ballistic missile, the DF-17, appeared in China's National Day parade in 2019.[9] It is not billed as an ASBM, but with a sleek warhead shaped like a lifting body, it shows the military's continuing interest in atmospheric manoeuvrability.

The only way an outside observer will know for certain how well the DF-21D and its successors work is if they are used operationally.

If that happens, the world is either in the early stages of a global conflagration, or several chapters deep into one.

Carrier strike groups remain a staple of US naval force projection, able to hit any corner of the world at short notice with overwhelming force. Although China has two carriers in service, neither is nuclear powered nor uses catapults for launch, making them more of a training tool than a weapon. For years, US war planners took for granted that American naval power could operate unimpeded anywhere on Earth and deliver pain as needed. If a missile can sweep that option off the board, it changes the balance of power not just in Asia, but across the globe as other countries scramble for such systems.

China is the only country to build large numbers of ballistic missiles to threaten enemy fleets. The United States is the only power on Earth with more than a single nuclear-powered aircraft carrier. Neither fact seems likely to change in the near future, putting both countries on what may be a collision course of doctrine and technology.

That makes the development, deployment and threat posed by the DF-21D crucial to study. The outcome of the next great power conflict might hinge upon whether this missile truly is a carrier killer.

1
STRIKING AT THE HEART OF THE FLEET

The DF-21D and its brethren might not exist if no one had thought to try flying a rickety biplane off boards bolted to the deck of an aging cruiser more than 100 years ago. That successful experiment led to a decades-long proliferation of aircraft carriers that, in the minds of People's Liberation Army planners, led to an untenable situation: American warships sailing unchallenged just off the Chinese mainland. It was a collision of strategies that was in some ways inevitable.

Genesis of the Aircraft Carrier

Since the Second World War, the aircraft carrier has occupied the centre of US Navy strategy – the ultimate conventional offensive weapon. A modern aircraft carrier embarks squadrons of aircraft capable of delivering tons of high explosives over thousands of miles, and that can attack targets in the air, on the sea, and on land. Along with strike aircraft, they also carry helicopters for support, as well as airborne early warning aircraft. The menagerie of

firepower is unparalleled at sea, and on land matched only by an airfield.

In 1910, Eugene Ely became the first pilot to fly an aircraft off a warship when he launched a biplane off the deck of the reconfigured cruiser USS *Birmingham*. (Public domain)

Sailors loading Ely's 50 hp. Curtiss Model D Pusher biplane aboard USS *Birmingham*. (US Navy)

Imperial Japanese Navy aircraft carrier *Hōshō*. (Public domain)

With their nuclear powerplants, each ship can stay at sea indefinitely, only reliant on the shore for provisions, aircraft fuel, and munitions, much of which they can receive while under way.

Although it is a literal and figurative big target for adversaries, no carrier has been sunk since the Second World War. Many weapons developments during the Cold War – super-quiet attack submarines and long-range anti-ship missiles, for instance – arose out of the simple, unflagging desire to send an aircraft carrier to the bottom.

But the carrier's elevation to the clenched fist of the fleet has happened in an eyeblink, relative to the history of naval warfare. The

US Navy kicked things off at the beginning of the twentieth century, when it retrofitted an aging cruiser for an experiment that would revolutionize sea power. Shipwrights at Norfolk Navy Yard fitted the 423-foot USS *Birmingham* with an 83-foot wooden platform, and embarked an American stunt pilot, Eugene B. Ely, along with his 50-horsepower Curtiss Model D Pusher biplane.[1] On 14 November 1910, the ship got under way and travelled from Norfolk to the Chesapeake Bay, anchoring off the coast to make history. Ely launched his plane from the improvised deck at 3:17 p.m., making

Royal Navy aircraft carrier HMS *Hermes*. (US Navy)

US Navy aircraft carrier USS *Langley* (CV-1). (US Navy)

The race to perfect the art of operating combat aircraft from these ships dovetailed directly into the Second World War, when Japan's carriers conducted the first massed aircraft carrier-led attack on a day that would 'live in infamy.' The strike at the home turf of the US Pacific Fleet involved hundreds of carrier aircraft bombing and strafing a fleet bottled up in Pearl Harbor. US carriers – even then, the focus of an enemy's firepower – were at sea, however, and would survive to fight another day.

In a stroke, the value of carriers was no longer theoretical, but a proven commodity.

From Curiosity to Strategic Linchpin

The Second World War in the Pacific is often thought of as a war of aircraft carriers, with the reign of the battleship brought to an end at Pearl Harbor and off the coast of Malaya, where Japanese aircraft sank the only Royal Navy ships in the Far East. In reality, only five carrier-to-carrier battles took place in the entire war, all between May and October 1942.[3] But the ship's flexibility saw it play a role in many other aspects of

him the first pilot, and the US Navy the first naval force, to launch an aircraft from a warship.[2]

The first purpose-built aircraft carriers came soon after, but they were not American.

The Imperial Japanese Navy's *Hōshō* was completed in 1922, 13 months before the Royal Navy completed its first carrier, the HMS *Hermes*.

the war, from escort duties to supporting amphibious invasions of islands across the Pacific theatre. That versatility meant that between the 1920s to war's end, the US had built 161 carriers of eight different classes, from the larger fleet carrier to the light escort variant, and their role as the centre of fleet operations had been cemented.

The US relied on carrier aviation for operations on the Korean Peninsula, attacking targets not just at sea or on shore, but deep

The Imperial Japanese Navy ship *Wakamiya* was the first operational aircraft carrier, launching seaplanes in combat in 1914. (Public domain)

The USS *Enterprise*, CV-6, was a key part of the United States' Second World War carrier fleet, fighting in the Battle of Midway and taking part in the Doolittle Raid on Tokyo. (US Navy)

The USS *Constellation* was one of several US carriers to support airstrikes and air superiority missions during the Vietnam War. The war showed planners that aircraft launched from the sea could be used effectively deep inside enemy territory. (US Navy)

inland, providing air support that doctrinally had always come from land-based aircraft. One of the most famous Hollywood treatments of the Korean War, *The Bridges of Toko-Ri*, provides an unrivalled look at the perilous missions flown from US fleet carriers during the conflict, and highlights the fact that carriers were increasingly useful for supporting operations past the shoreline – a novel idea at the war's start. As aircraft technology improved, bombing sorties could be flown deeper and deeper inland, and with heavier bomb loads.

Even before the Korean War, carriers had become behemoths. The 45,000-ton Midway class, laid down shortly after the Second World War, served through to the 1990s. But USS *Forrestal*, first in the Forrestal-class, kicked off the age of the supercarrier when it was commissioned in 1955. By the time the US was fully invested in the Vietnam War, carriers were 25 percent larger and 100 feet longer, with the angled flight deck that still defines the carrier's shape today. Carrying dozens of jet aircraft and tons of munitions, carriers struck targets all over Vietnam. With the North Vietnamese Navy almost non-existent, the carriers were essentially unchallenged at sea and

provided moveable, invulnerable air bases for strike aircraft. In one of the most poignant photographs of the war, US personnel pushed helicopters into the sea from the deck of an aircraft carrier used to receive one of the last refugee flights out of South Vietnam.

Harnessing the Power of the Atom

Around then, the first nuclear aircraft carrier arrived on the scene. The USS *Enterprise*, CVN-65, was at the time the longest warship ever built and marked the advent of modern carrier operations. The follow-on class, the Nimitz-class, entered service in 1975 and was slightly smaller than *Enterprise*. Most of those ships are still in service in 2021. These modern fleet carriers displace at least 100,000 tons and are 330 meters long. With a full complement of sailors and the accompanying air wing, each ship embarks nearly 6,000 people. But nuclear power is what makes them stand out, not their gargantuan dimensions. The ships can hit over 30 knots and, more important, can stay under way indefinitely, constrained only

The nuclear-powered USS *Enterprise*, CVN-65, was the first US aircraft carrier to have a nuclear reactor. The powerplant enabled it to stay at sea indefinitely, as long as it had enough supplies for its crew and aircraft. (US Navy)

Alfa-class submarines, designed in the Soviet Union in the 1960s, were state-of-the-art weapons meant to counter the United States' growing surface warfare dominance, driven by its aircraft carriers. (US Navy)

The Tu-22M Backfire bomber, first fielded during the Cold War and still flying in the 2020s, was meant to attack US aircraft carriers with weapons such as the Kh-22 anti-ship missile. (US Department of Defense)

by the other supplies it needs – boring stuff like food, water, fuel and weapons.

By the time the Cold War ended, carrier operations were crucial to the operating style of the US Navy and US military more broadly. The Soviet Union, aghast at the huge price tag of a nuclear-powered carrier (roughly $10 billion each), took an asymmetric response, developing a powerful submarine fleet and long-range anti-ship missiles to counter the threat.

The Centrepiece of American Expeditionary Warfare

Every major US military operation in recent memory has involved US carriers. Operation El Dorado Canyon in Libya in 1986, Praying Mantis in the Persian Gulf in 1988, Operation Urgent Fury in Grenada in 1983 – all incorporated power projected from supercarriers. The Navy's carriers carried out more than 13,000 sorties against the regime of Saddam Hussein in 1991.[4] When the US military's attention returned to Iraq and the Middle East a decade later, naval aircraft often led the way with precision bombing.

Task Force 155, centred around three US aircraft carriers, the USS *John F. Kennedy,* the USS *Saratoga* and the USS *America,* was a key part of US airpower during Operation Desert Storm in 1991. (US Navy)

Operation El Dorado Canyon, the bombing raid against Libya in 1986, is best known for the use of F-111 bombers. But aircraft from the USS *America* (CV-66) supported the raid by patrolling for Libyan aircraft and suppressing air defences. (US Navy)

Carriers also occupy a sweet spot in popular culture, thanks to their size and photogenic load of sleek fighters. The 1980s were arguably the peak of Hollywood's love affair with the aircraft carrier in the form of *Top Gun.* The movie's real star, USS *Enterprise,* would later also appear in the screen adaptation of Tom Clancy's *The Hunt for Red October.*[5][6]

So it should be clear that carriers now represent not just the biggest club in a navy's arsenal, but also a psychological symbol of power. Even China's rudimentary carriers, based on Soviet Cold War designs, get the country's citizenry excited with images of flight deck operations.[7] That makes them a focal point for adversaries.

What Does the Carrier Bring to the Table? Everything!

In its position at the centre of US naval strategy, the aircraft carrier fills four key roles: generating maritime awareness, neutralizing enemy naval power, raiding and strike warfare, and providing a floating airfield.[8] The carrier's embarked air wing provides the first three, with scouting functions and ability to deliver bombs and missiles many hundreds of miles from the carrier. All four functions require the carrier to be able to launch and recover aircraft. Without that, the carrier becomes a liability, a floating hotel with mediocre room service and a limited ability to defend itself.

The guided-missile cruiser USS *Shiloh* (CG-67), the USS *Ronald Reagan* (CVN-76), and the Singaporean Navy frigate RSS *Intrepid* (FFS-69) steam through the South China Sea. USS *Ronald Reagan* is the flagship of Carrier Strike Group 5. (US Navy)

The Victor-class submarine was another example of the Soviet Union turning to high-tech undersea weapons to combat US surface fleets. (US Navy)

Defending the Carrier

As a high-value asset, each deployed carrier is protected by a formidable ring of defences. A mixture of guided-missile destroyers and cruisers provide protection against enemy submarines, aircraft, and missiles. But a shrinking US Navy offers less and less defence for each carrier. Carrier battle groups a generation ago included twice as many ships as a carrier strike group of today.[9] Those same battlegroups also carried up to 30 percent more aircraft. Advances in technology can offset some of that gap, but quantity does have a quality all its own. As Senator Sam Nunn once noted, 'At some point, technology fails to offset mass.'[10]

Decades of unchallenged maritime superiority lulled the US Navy into a false sense of security, building fewer numbers of exquisite platforms with superior capabilities. In a larger conflict against a peer, however, the loss of even one of these sophisticated ships or aircraft will be felt more keenly. Even so, the modern carrier strike group is still an unmatched force in terms of the combat power it brings to bear.

The standard air wing within the carrier strike group (CSG) offers a panoply of tactical aircraft capabilities across the spectrum of warfare – airborne early warning, defensive counterair, airborne command and control, electronic attack, anti-surface warfare, and strike. With its embarked helicopters it can provide a modicum of anti-submarine warfare and search and rescue protection for the strike group as well. Those capabilities come from a mix of approximately 60 aircraft, though most prevalent is the F-18 Super Hornet. In future years, F-35s and uncrewed aircraft will be joining the fleet.

So as China's global interests have expanded alongside its expansive claims in the South China Sea, its planners' attention has zeroed in on US carriers. As keen observers of the American way of war, Chinese strategists know that any effort to stop their advances will be spearheaded by the US Navy's aircraft carriers.

Reports of the Carrier's Death are Greatly Exaggerated

Some have said that the Chinese anti-ship ballistic missile program portends the end of the aircraft carrier as the centrepiece of naval

The USS *Theodore Roosevelt* Carrier Strike Group steams through the South China Sea in formation with the USS *Nimitz* Carrier Strike Group. (US Navy)

The USS *Gerald R. Ford* is the lead ship in the United States' latest class of multibillion-dollar nuclear-powered aircraft carriers, a sign that their place in the US Navy is undiminished. (US Navy)

warfare. Headlines proclaim that 'The Navy Must Accept That the Aircraft Carrier Age is Ending.'[11] But the US Navy is investing in a new class of ship to replace the Nimitz-class: American shipyards have launched two nuclear-powered Ford-class ships and show no signs of turning away from the statutory requirement that holds the Navy to fielding no fewer than 11 carriers in active service. Meanwhile China, despite having supposedly sounded the death knell for aircraft carriers with its missile programs, is now building its own conventionally powered aircraft carriers,[12] and some sources claim nuclear-powered carriers may be next.[13]

China, like other nations, has invested heavily in 'ordinary' weapons that can attack carriers, such as submarines and anti-ship missiles. It has grown its submarine fleet and added nuclear-powered models, and its cruise missile arsenal offers formidable striking power on its own, especially with some of these anti-ship rounds based on its man-made Spratly Island outposts.

But China's highest-profile threat to the aircraft carrier is now something more exotic: a missile that spends most of its flight in space and can strike thousands of kilometres away from the mainland – beyond even the reach of a carrier's strike fighters. The

DF-21D seeks to bypass a carrier strike group's thicket of defensive capabilities altogether, plunging in from space and speeding by countermeasures developed for much different types of weapons. Designed to counter the American carrier from a position of weakness – the US, in 2022, has no conventional ballistic missile forces to speak of – the PRC's anti-ship ballistic missiles were originally the ace-in-the-hole weapon of a weak, land-based military. Now, however, the DF-21D is part of an integrated force composed of a powerful navy, an advanced air force, and the world's largest shore-based ballistic and cruise missile arsenal. Within that combined force, the DF-21D presents an unprecedented threat, or the potential for one, to the keystone of American naval power. Some have presented it as an unstoppable silver bullet; others have posited that it is a bluff. In either case, it has necessitated a sweeping (and at times panicked) re-examination of how the US Navy operates at sea. After 30 years of unchallenged command of the waves, as well as freedom to launch attacks on land from undisputed littorals, the US Navy must now reckon with a weapon that aims to gut its very theory of victory.

2

A REVOLUTIONARY SYMBOL

When many carrier-borne aircraft are used in continuous air strikes against our coast, in order to halt the powerful air raids, the enemy's core carrier should be struck as with a 'heavy hammer.[1]

The weapons of the People's Liberation Army Rocket Force are a symbol of the Chinese Communist Party's dedication to driving the US out of the centre of the Indo-Pacific security network and carving out a sphere of influence dominated by Beijing. In many ways, the DF-21D is the embodiment of this attitude:

The Luda-class destroyer was developed in the 1950s but did not sail until the 1970s. Through most of the twentieth century, China's navy was made up of outdated foreign equipment and domestic vessels far behind the state of the art. (US Navy)

There is more potent symbolism in this missile than any other weapon in the Chinese arsenal. This is the missile that really does potentially encroach on US capability to deploy military power close to Chinese shores. It significantly raises the risks and costs.[2]

The symbolism is aimed at audiences inside and outside of the country. The Chinese Communist Party regularly presents the DF-21D as an internal sign of strength to the Chinese people – and an implicit threat to foreign forces seeking to encroach on the country's sovereignty.

Standing Up

In 1949, Mao Zedong stood in Tiananmen Square before gathered multitudes to establish the foundation of the central government of the People's Republic of China. A quote commonly attributed to the Great Helmsman supposedly proclaimed that 'the Chinese people have stood up,' proclaiming that the so-called Century of Shame and Humiliation was over and a new state was rising from the ashes to reclaim the legacy of Chinese civilization.[3] From its ignominious defeat in the Opium War of 1840 until that moment, China had been at the

Mao Zedong announces the founding of the People's Republic of China in 1949, proclaiming that the Chinese people had 'stood up' and would never again be humiliated. (Hou Bo)

Jianghu-I class frigate as photographed by a US Navy P-3C Orion crew. The class entered service in the 1970s and most were decommissioned in 2012. Several remain in service with the PLAN and China Coast Guard. (Public domain)

Two FA-18C Hornets of Strike Fighter Squadron 74 fly above the Forrestal-class aircraft carrier USS *Saratoga* (CV-60), making a hard turn to starboard during Operation Desert Shield, 4 November 1990. (US Navy)

mercy of its tormentors; with his words, that began to change. The sentiment is echoed today in the rumble of trucks bearing ballistic missiles through the streets of Beijing every year on the anniversary of Mao's speech. They are a symbol and a signal as much as a weapon.

Although the Chinese people may have stood up in 1949, their knees were wobbling and the ground beneath them was shaky. Already reeling from the collapse of the Qing dynasty, a decade of war with Japan and the blood-soaked internecine civil war left China staggering just as it plunged into the Korean War in 1950. In subsequent decades, China was an embattled, weak state. It was surrounded by unfriendly states, and its border with Russia was hotly contested. Often a pariah in international affairs due to its profligate support for anti-capitalist revolutionaries the world over, for the brutality of the Cultural Revolution, and for the slaughter committed against protesters at Tiananmen Square in 1989, China's security at home was the ruling Communist Party's primary focus. As with most inwardly focused regimes, China's maritime power withered at expense of its land forces, the enormous People's Liberation Army. Even as recently as the 1990s, the People's Liberation Army Navy was a rickety, brown-water force made up mostly of Soviet-era antiques, incapable of deterring an attack from the sea or patrolling more than a stone's throw from shore.

Learning from Traumatic Experience

The DF-21D was developed to address the shortfall in conventional naval capability that allowed the United States to sail two nuclear aircraft carriers near the Taiwan Strait unchallenged, an event that still looms large in the shameful back rooms of the CCP's memory. The Third Taiwan Strait Crisis of 1995–96 is often correctly cited as a catalyst for China's development of ASBMs, but the regime's insecurity about its relationship with the United States did not

begin there. Rather, the origins of this security dilemma lie far from China's borders – in the oil-rich sands of Kuwait.

The American campaign to liberate Kuwait from Saddam Hussein's 1991 invasion caught Chinese leaders by surprise. Not the action itself, which was clearly telegraphed, but the speed and ferocity with which it was carried out. Watching a formidable Iraqi military, among the world's largest and in some ways similar to the People's Liberation Army, crushed in a matter of weeks by a lightning-fast combination of air power, networked combatants, and sophisticated smart weapons was a cold dose of reality for China's Central Military Commission. With the sting of the PLA's 1979 marginally successful war against Vietnam still fresh in their minds, the modern military power on display during Desert Storm was almost unimaginable. The concepts ensconced within the Revolution in Military Affairs – networked platforms, advanced sensors, and precision weapons – were distant dreams for the PLA, which was still weighed down by Cold War technology and doctrine. The obliteration of Saddam's war machine was as instructive as it was shocking: the Military Commission received a free look at the American playbook and the future of warfare, at the Iraqi Army's expense.

Just a few years later, China's military planners got an even closer look. In March 1996, the People's Liberation Army fired several ballistic missiles into the waters around Taiwan during a period of high cross-strait tensions. One American carrier, the USS *Independence*, was already in the area, and it was subsequently joined by USS *Nimitz*. The two carriers, with their associated battle groups, were dispatched to within 100 miles of the Taiwan Strait. US National Security Advisor Anthony Lake publicly warned Beijing of 'grave consequences' if there were any overt aggression toward Taiwan itself. To Chinese leaders, the historical parallel to the foreign navies of the nineteenth century that plied Chinese waters unchallenged

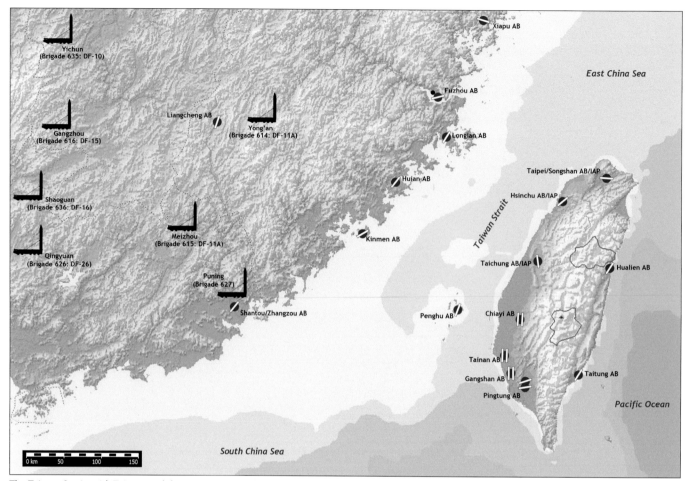

The Taiwan Strait, with Taiwan and the nearest parts of mainland China, the most important air bases on either side, and the nearest missile units of the PLA. (Map by Tom Cooper)

during the so-called Century of Shame and Humiliation was undeniable. The US response to the Third Taiwan Strait Crisis tapped into internalized trauma. Once again, half a century after Mao's announcement, China was unable to challenge a foreign invader, even when one of the country's core interests, and national sovereignty, were at stake. The United States, in its unipolar moment of unchallenged global power, flaunted its unrivalled strength in the maritime domain under China's nose, and the world was watching. The humiliation has been intentionally ingrained since then in the collective memory of the Chinese Communist Party.

An Iraqi Type 69 tank – designed and built in China – burns in the early days of Operation Desert Storm in 1991. The swift, decisive victory by US and allied forces in that war was one of several events that spurred China to focus on modernising its military and moving away from large ground forces as a deterrent. (US Department of Defense)

The USS *Nimitz* (left) and USS *Independence* sail with the USS *Port Royal*, a guided-missile cruiser, months after the Third Taiwan Strait Crisis. The two carriers led the US response to China's testing a series of missiles in the waters off Taiwan in 1996. (US Navy)

These are the events in the observable foreground. Behind the scenes, China had already begun its strategic transformation after the first Gulf War. China's doctrinal focus shifted significantly in the early 1990s, away from the paradigms of 'People's War' and 'Limited War' to 'Limited War Under High Tech Conditions.'[4] Being late to this latest Revolution in Military Affairs – a periodic sea change in doctrine and technology as the world's militaries struggle to address future threats – meant that China now had to consider its defence from a position of weakness relative to the United States. Reliance on massed infantry attacks or insurgency would not counter US capabilities at sea, nor were they likely to be an effective deterrent for anything short of a full-scale invasion.

Then, in 1999, a third incident erased any doubt for China's Politburo and Central Military Commission that urgent changes were needed. On the night of 7 May, during the NATO air campaign against Slobodan Milosevic's regime, American B-2 Spirit bombers dropped five precision-guided Joint Direct Attack Munitions (JDAMs) on the Chinese embassy in Belgrade, killing three journalists and wounding 20 Chinese embassy employees.[5] The American apology was immediate, and the bombing was quickly declared an accident. Subsequent investigation revealed that the bombs were dropped on the building intentionally; the embassy had been mistaken for a Serbian military facility and wrongly classified as a target, based on out-of-date maps and a faulty targeting process.[6] China, however, was not placated. Outrage erupted, and not just in the halls of government. Hundreds of demonstrators, with government backing, gathered in the streets to protest outside the US embassy in Beijing and its other consulates across the country. Vice-President Hu Jintao even addressed the outflow of anti-

US vitriol, stating that the protests 'fully reflect the Chinese people's great fury at the atrocity of the embassy attacks by NATO and the Chinese people's strong patriotism.'[7]

Many believed that the strike had been intentional and refused to accept the idea that dumb targeting had led smart bombs to be dropped on the wrong target. Adding insult to injury was the reinforcement of the fact that if a foreign power wanted to try a similar intervention in or near China, the People's Liberation Army had no way of preventing it. Much like Desert Storm, China was now watching another, albeit smaller, military with equipment similar to its own being dismantled by ferocious displays of US airpower and precision munitions.

What the Enemy Fears Most

The Chinese Communist Party's General Secretary, Jiang Zemin, responded to the tragedy in Belgrade with the New-Type High-Technology Weapons Plan, otherwise known as the 995 Program. Numbered 995 for May of 1999, the project was the embodiment of Jiang's guidance that 'Whatever the enemy fears most, that is what we should develop.'[8] Jiang's goal was to use asymmetric capabilities

Soldiers in protective gear withdraw after erecting a DF-21A medium-range ballistic missile system during a training exercise in 2018. (eng.chinamil.com.cn)

15

to negate American advantages in technology – developing novel strategies and systems rather than trying to beat the US military at its own expensive game.

The emphasis on this kind of strategy is a common thread in the fundamental texts of Chinese strategic thought. From the oft-quoted Sun Tzu's advice to avoid strong points and attack the enemy where he is weakest, to Mao Zedong's treatises on People's War, focus on asymmetry dominates the rhetorical battlefield. Even the Chinese term for these asymmetric capabilities, *shashoujian*, or 'assassin's mace,' has become popularized within the US defence community when speaking of China's defence. With roots in Tang Empire-era warfare, the term *shashoujian* can be understood as a close-guarded, powerful capability that, in modern terms, encompasses both hardware, software, and doctrine[9]. Even before the attack in Belgrade, General Fu Quanyou, vice chairman of the Central Military Commission, addressed China's need for *shashoujian*, opining that 'To defeat a better equipped enemy with inferior equipment in the context of high-technology, we [the PRC] should rely upon high-quality personnel, superior operational methods, and high-quality *shashoujian* weapons.'[10] Care should be taken not to exoticize this term, or the pursuit of asymmetric means of warfare – the major Axis powers, for example, invested heavily in novel weapons during the Second World War, and both the United States and Soviet Union experimented with weird and wild systems during the Cold War, searching for an advantage. It is also important to understand that China developed the DF-21D specifically to counter what Beijing saw as the centre of gravity of the American expeditionary warfighting machine: the nuclear-powered aircraft carrier. Any discussion of the DF-21D that did not address the confluence of popular elements of Chinese strategic thought, historical background and military need would be incomplete.

China's Age-Old Problem

The strategic circumstances that found China struggling to find ways to fend off a serious challenge on its periphery are not new to Chinese leaders. China's strategic situation has long been defined by a need to ensure security at home despite more powerful enemies lurking on its extensive borders. In modern Chinese history, Mao Zedong discussed the concept of active defence, or offensive defence, in his 1936 *Problems of Strategy in China's Revolutionary War*, which was a reflection on the Red Army's experience in the Second Revolutionary Civil War against the Kuomintang. In his words, active defence can also be thought of as 'defence through decisive

engagements.'[11] An episode from China's past brutally illustrates this concept. As the Cultural Revolution raged in China, the Communist Party lighted upon the 'unequal treaties' levied upon the Qing government in the nineteenth century as a way to help whip up revolutionary fervour among their own population, much as the patriotic education campaign of the twenty-first century relies upon the century of humiliation as a motivating principle.[12] The status of the otherwise unimportant Zhenbao Island on the Ussuri River, and whether it belonged to the Soviet Union or China, became a point of tension, with Soviet and PLA troops frequently facing off in minor confrontations that occasionally involved shoving matches and fistfights. Then, on 2 March 1969, a Soviet patrol confronted approximately 30 Chinese troops that had crossed the frozen river. According to Soviet accounts, the Chinese troops had hidden weapons, opening fire with submachine guns on their unsuspecting adversaries. Overwhelming fire exploded from camouflaged foxholes where several hundred more PLA troops had concealed themselves overnight. The Soviets reported 30 killed in the initial fighting, and the Zhenbao Island incident escalated rapidly, with both sides reinforcing their positions and employing heavy armor. Soviet forces used rocket artillery to drive the PLA back. Hundreds were killed in the ensuing battles and despite a cease-fire declared after two weeks, threats of a nuclear exchange persisted for months afterward.[13] At the time, each side was quick to blame the other for initiating the border bloodshed. However, contemporary historians from both Russia and China have reached a general consensus that Mao conceived the incident as an act of active defence. In 1969, he was concerned that the recently announced Brezhnev Doctrine, which proclaimed Soviet willingness to intervene militarily in Socialist states to ensure a steady hand remained at the helm, might be used as justification for Moscow to intervene in China as it had in Czechoslovakia the previous year. To ward off such a possibility, Mao elected to teach the Soviets 'a bitter lesson,' a reminder of China's resolve.[14]

Mao initiated the border conflict under the assumption that the PLA's overwhelming numerical superiority would dissuade potential Soviet adventurism in the future. The subsequent escalation caught the Chinese off-guard, as did the subsequent threats of a nuclear exchange that the Chinese were unprepared to match. Zhenbao Island now belongs to China, the attack did appear to temper Soviet appetites for further conflict, and the idea of active defence still features at the forefront of Chinese military thinking, as evidenced by its inclusion in the 2019 Defense White Paper.[15] But the messy conclusion of the incident highlights the unpredictability inherent in such a strategy – a reminder that even in the best-laid plans, the enemy always gets a vote.

Active Defence

The DF-21D and other anti-ship ballistic missiles exemplify this school of thought, which the US Department of Defense describes as 'The employment of limited offensive action and counterattacks to deny a contested area or position to the enemy.'[16] Though Beijing may regularly stress the

A screenshot of the People's Liberation Army Rocket Force's first promotional video, featuring ballistic missiles on transporter-erector launchers. (eng.chinamil.com.cn)

Military parades, including the massive annual National Day celebration, are often a way for China to showcase new weapons such as anti-ship ballistic missiles or hypersonic glide weapons. (US Department of Defense)

defensive nature of its missile force, the defensive strategy involving these weapons uses them for pre-emptive strikes designed to teach a costly lesson. Repeated claims such as 'the PLA will not fire the first shot, but the DF-21D and DF-26B may be the second' imply Chinese restraint and attempt to paint the US as the belligerent.[17] However, closer examination of Chinese doctrine reveals that the enemy's first shot might not be a shot at all. Phrasing like 'as soon as the enemy splits and invades China's territory, severely harming China's interests' is laid out as 'equivalent to firing the first shot at China at the strategic level,'[18] seemingly reinforcing Beijing's willingness, or even intent, to strike first, in response to trespassing in what it sees as its territory, on land or sea. This is what some analysts might refer to as a non-linear approach to naval warfare – unconstrained

by battle lines or geography and dissimilar to the way Western militaries view the road to war.[19] Mao's legacy of viewing active defence as principally about 'breaking the enemy's 'encirclement and suppression'[20] is still a valid lens for observing Chinese military strategy, and repeated, vehement objections from Beijing regarding American attempts to 'contain'[21] and 'encircle'[22] China should be understood in this context.

Anti-Access Area Denial

China aims to neutralize its primary opponent's most valuable conventional weapons with so-called Anti-Access/Area Denial (A2AD) weapons, theoretically capable of targeting ships and bases thousands of miles from China before they can get within striking

An H-6K bomber takes off from an airfield in China. The bombers offer a way for China to project power – in the form of air-launched anti-ship missiles – at sea far from its shores. (eng.chinamil.com.cn/)

A carrier strike group, seen here organized in close formation around the nuclear-powered USS *George Washington* (CVN-73), involves multiple surface ships and sometimes submarines. In ordinary operations, the ships are arranged far from the carrier, providing security, sensors and added firepower. (US Navy)

distance of anything crucial. The magic of maritime A2AD is that it does not create any effects in peacetime: there are no tangible, impassable barriers, no minefields or barbed wire. It does, however, raise the risks and costs of otherwise ordinary actions such as sailing warships in international waters, and vastly complicates planning for any potential conflict between China and an adversary at sea.[23] The DF-21D, for instance – if it works as advertised – could create very large flaming holes in ships that venture inside the First Island Chain, which traces down from Japan, through Taiwan and the Philippines. This 'A2AD bubble' then becomes unsafe for operations and any high-value asset, like an aircraft carrier, requires escort by ships capable of ballistic missile defence.

In theory, China's defensive umbrella would spring into being to deter US intervention during an invasion of Taiwan or another contingency in which Beijing seeks to consolidate gains while keeping the United States at arm's length.[24] Chinese official sources refer to this concept as 'counterintervention' – the somewhat dizzying idea of intervening to prevent an intervention, which exists as a subset of China's active defence paradigm.[25] At one time, this strategy was thought to cover the 'three seas' – Yellow, East China, and South China, or perhaps the waters enclosed by the First Island Chain. However, as China's missile capabilities expand, it seems clear that Beijing's ambitions are somewhat more wide-reaching. But until the shooting starts, the bubble only exists in theory. That is where the mystique long surrounding the DF-21D and its capabilities is most useful to China.

Changing Threat Perceptions

With a road-mobile missile capable of threatening the crown jewel of the American fleet, China rocketed forward in US Navy threat perceptions in Asia over the past decade. Suddenly a navy that was a unsteady mix of Soviet-era relics and of brown- and green-water attack craft was backed by a potentially devastating capability spearing down from the heavens. The spectre of Chinese anti-access/area denial (A2AD) quickly took root in Western planning. The truly remarkable part is that the entire concept rested on capabilities that existed in reputation only. Until late 2020, the DF-21D had never, so far as unclassified sources can corroborate, been tested against

a moving target at sea. It was only during the period of US-China tensions during the waning days of the Trump administration that a retired People's Liberation Army general claimed that both the DF-21D and DF-26 had been used to strike targets at sea during a Chinese joint exercise.[26] But even that announcement illustrated the intentionally curated ambiguity surrounding these missiles. The source – retired General Wang Xiangsui, not an official spokesman, but one thought to be part of the inner circles of Chinese strategy – is also notable as the author of a modern classic in Chinese strategic thinking. His book, *Unrestricted Warfare*, unequivocally advocates use of asymmetric tools to undermine and defeat technologically superior opponents.[27] Who better to perpetuate the mythos surrounding this strategic deterrent?

ASBMs in Modern Chinese Defence Strategy

Modern Chinese defence strategy, as described by PLA research professors in the *Science of Military Strategy*, presents a strong doctrinal preference for deterrence, with active defence as the first response if deterrence fails.[28] As described in the International Institute for Strategic Studies Asia-Pacific Regional Security Assessment in 2017, this strategy hinges upon China's ability to influence American perceptions of risk: the likelihood of intervention by the United States 'depends on this trade-off [analysis] between war risks and costs.'[29]

In the event that Beijing is unable to dissuade the United States from intervention, land-based missiles, including ASBMs, would be the preferred tool for controlling the near seas and preventing Beijing from being surrounded. The deep-rooted fear of encirclement drives strategy for a traditionally land-based Chinese military previously traumatized by its inability to resist maritime incursions.

'For the PLAN, near-seas active defence requires a minimum being able to hold enemy forces at risk within certain parts of the near seas and their immediate approaches, and ideally to hold opposing forces at risk throughout China's immediate periphery.'[30] That assessment was in 2017. In the space of only a few years, China has become much more confident in how it shapes outward-facing messaging based on ASBMs.

The USS *Ronald Reagan* (CVN-76), forward deployed in Japan as part of the US 7th Fleet, transits the South China Sea. (US Navy)

State Media and Signalling

Chinese media commonly hold up the DF-21D and its successor, the DF-26, as powerful tools of the Communist Party, ready to punish the United States for its many offenses committed against the Chinese people. The Global Times, a nationalist Chinese outlet commonly seen as a testbed for more radical or confrontational messages, has referenced these so-called 'carrier killers' in at least 30 articles and op-eds between 2011 and 2020. Seventeen were released in 2020, as tensions between the Trump administration and the CCP ratcheted higher and higher. With titles like 'PLA Rocket Force launches DF-26 'aircraft carrier killer' missile in fast-reaction drills'[31] and 'Hopefully, 'carrier killer' missiles would never be used in the South China Sea,' these obvious signals are meant for an American audience. And the message gets more pointed – 'But which regional country that has territorial disputes with China owns aircraft carriers? If the PLA really launched missiles into the South China Sea, does this have anything to do with those countries?'[32] In short, its neighbours have nothing to fear, as long as they do not get involved in the aircraft carrier business. This would seem to lend credence to the ASBMs' reputation as a signalling tool, as well as a weapon. As the CCP looks forward to a future defined by 'informationised warfare,' its increasingly sophisticated missile programs are held up as symbols of China's rising power and strength on the world stage.[33]

The DF-21D, and China's ASBM programs more broadly, also represent an element of China's national position on international law, which increasingly resembles an endorsement of the legal principle of *mare clausum*, or a closed sea, seeking to 'acculturate the West to the idea of external seas becoming internal waters.'[34] Indeed the leverage offered by ASBMs is commonly invoked in China's attempts at subverting the idea of *mare liberum*, or the free sea, as Beijing slowly but surely advances its campaign to control the waters within its Nine-Dash Line, an expansive, theoretical boundary based on a single Chinese map from the 1940s.

Chinese Dream, American Nightmare?

General Secretary Xi Jinping has described his vision for China as a 'Chinese Dream,' a national rejuvenation and end to his predecessors' dedication to Deng Xiaoping's maxim of hiding and biding.[35] Under Xi, China's defence posture has become robust and, in many areas, confrontational, challenging the United States' decades of near-complete domination of the sea in the Indo-Pacific. Framing the Chinese Dream as a resumption of China's role as a Great Power, as well as a fulfilment of the Qin Dynasty proverb (also adopted by today's CCP) 'Wealthy State, Strong Army,'[36] has seen concerted efforts to amplify convenient vignettes from China's history as well as tap into a rich vein of Chinese strategic thought, as well as deep-seated national trauma and resentment. Centuries of history offer valuable context for China's ASBM program – from its age-old security dilemmas to what it means for the country's modern nationalism. The DF-21D stands out as a symbol of China's ambitions as well as a potentially fearsome weapon. Ignoring that context to focus on the missiles' technology could put an adversary on a miscalculated path to conflict, and catastrophe.

3

DEATH FROM ABOVE

The first operational ballistic missile – if one ignores unguided versions like the ones spraying a red glare over Fort McHenry hundreds of years ago – took flight in 1944, in the form of the German V-2, which used simple inertial guidance to land within several kilometres of its intended target. It was fuelled with alcohol and liquid oxygen just before flight and was fired from a mobile

A DF-21D and its launcher. The missile uses solid fuel, which means it can be fired with little preparation beyond stabilizing the launcher and programming coordinates. (Office of Naval Intelligence)

launch platform. Steered by gyroscopes and guide fins, it arrived downrange at supersonic speed and delivered a 1,000-kilogram warhead several times larger than the typical aerial bomb of the era.

In the twenty-first century, the principles of a ballistic missile attack remain the same, even as improved technology makes the weapons bigger, more accurate and more deadly. There are new fuels, including solid rocket motors. Guidance to within tens of meters of a target is considered reasonable, even at ranges of 1,000 kilometres or more. Warheads are smaller by weight but use more energetic explosives (or nuclear reactions) and often are more effective because they can deliver their pain more precisely.[1]

One thing that has not changed is the easy part: the launch. If there is no time pressure or fear of, say, a hostile airstrike, the rocket can be programmed for flight at the crew's leisure. If it is on a mobile launcher – as the DF-21D is – the truck will be oriented to the correct azimuth and stabilized with jacks. After that it is just a matter of pushing a button from a safe distance[2].

Some modern missiles, such as North Korea's HS-15 ICBM,[3] need to be fuelled before launch. This introduces more failure points – fuel trucks can be destroyed, and dangerous chemicals can harm crews if they are not handled properly – and causes delays. The DF-21D skirts the complexities of fuelling in the field by using solid-fuel motors (manufactured by China Hexi Chemical and Machinery Corporation,[4] a subsidiary of the missile's manufacturer, China Aerospace Science and Industry Corporation), which require no prep time beyond making sure they are pointed in the right direction.

The hard part is figuring out where to aim; it is an intelligence, surveillance and reconnaissance (ISR) trick that becomes tougher at longer ranges. For distant targets that are on the move, an attack becomes a time-sensitive knife-juggling act. Unlike the V-2, which was sort of just flung in the general vicinity of Allied European population centres, a modern ballistic missile is expected to hit something specific: a facility, an artillery battery, a headquarters.

Or, in the case of an anti-ship ballistic missile, a warship. For fixed positions, geographical coordinates are enough; for targets on the move, fresh data and intelligence are needed to zero in.

The nuclear-armed Pershing II missile had a range of about 1,800 kilometres, and its steerable re-entry vehicle used radar and terrain maps to strike targets with a circular error probable of 30 meters. (US Army)

Old Problems, New Missiles

The DF-21D looks not much different than its less-sophisticated predecessors. No one has stood next to it holding a ruler, and there are no close-up images of the missile outside its canister, but comparing it with objects nearby during launches gives it rough dimensions of 10.7 meters long and 1.4 meters wide. It has two stages – a booster stage and an upper stage – and a range estimated at 1,500 kilometres.[5] It trundles through the countryside on a bus-sized vehicle that doubles as a launch platform and can drive for more than 100 kilometres without refuelling.

The missile and its successor, the DF-26, do not step outside the traditional ISR framework or push it far into a gee-whiz technological future. In fact, the more numerous DF-26 is in every way a 'normal' ballistic missile, except for its ability to quickly swap warhead sections: every DF-26 can carry a ballistic high-explosive payload, a nuclear weapon or an anti-ship re-entry vehicle.[6] Their growing numbers and longer range add a dimension to China's ASBM threat, but the fundamental capabilities of the RV section seem not much different from those of the DF-21D. An air-launched DF-21D variant is also in development, which would add range and flexibility to China's ASBM arsenal. All iterate on the possible, banking on a series of complex but workable connected steps. To

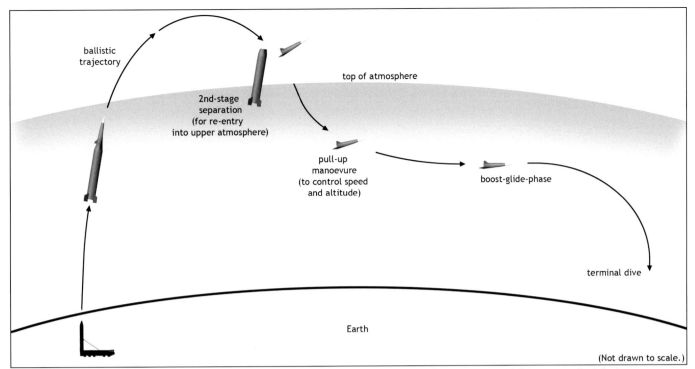

After re-entry, an ASBM descends into the atmosphere and then pulls up, 'flying' on a non-ballistic trajectory while its sensors look for its programmed target. (Diagram by Tom Cooper)

the extent there are any major advances, they are in the re-entry vehicle's sensors.[7] Their exact composition and capabilities are state secrets, of course. But whether the warhead sniffs out the target with radar, optical data, infrared or all three, the sensors must function in the harsh environment of re-entry and peer through or around any countermeasures thrown in their way.

Radar may be the most likely candidate for terminal guidance,[8] by virtue of being easier to function behind the protective shielding of a re-entry vehicle. This sort of mechanism is common in other systems, ranging from terrain navigation in nap-of-the-earth flying to other steerable re-entry vehicles, such as that of the US military's short-lived Pershing II missile.[9] The principles are simple: a transmitter blasts radio waves in front of the warhead. A receiver picks up those waves when they bounce off objects. A processor interprets those returns, gauging the distance between the warhead and the objects, and determining what those objects might be by comparing them to an onboard database. If it spots the correct shape – such as a 100,000-ton aircraft carrier – it sends signals to the re-entry vehicle's steering vanes, causing them to twitch and bend the warhead's flight path toward its target.[10] This is not all that different from the way TV-guided munitions or the radar systems onboard an anti-ship missile work.

The former Soviet Union experimented with a nuclear ASBM, the R-27K, in the 1960s and 1970s, fielding it for a time onboard a ballistic missile submarine.[11] Rather than active radar, it used passive radio guidance, homing in on the emissions of an aircraft carrier to score a hit – an easier proposition with a nuclear warhead.[12] But the problem of finding the carrier strike group to begin with proved too significant to make the missile much use relative to the much more numerous air-launched anti-ship missiles in the USSR's arsenal.

High and Hot

A re-entry vehicle for a weapon with the range of a DF-21D will hit the atmosphere at speeds of 20,000 to 25,000 kilometres per hour, depending on trajectory.[13] This is many times faster than even the fastest operational cruise missile, aircraft or even artillery shell. But

processors that can handle billions of operations per second can be found in commercial laptops, and there is little doubt that a radar-steered system could keep up, even at fresh-from-space speeds.

The re-entry vehicle will for a time be shrouded by superheated gas and bits of ablative material as it hits the atmosphere. This 'plasma sheath' is largely opaque to radio waves,[14] meaning the warhead can neither be steered by radar nor receive updated targeting data. The most obvious solution to this white-hot blindfold is to allow inertial (or coordinate-based) guidance to steer the re-entry vehicle while it performs a 'pull-up' manoeuvre, diverting from a ballistic atmospheric flight path onto a track that is nearly horizontal.[15] This bleeds off speed, dissipating the plasma as it flies toward the target area. The manoeuvre could also throw off any incoming interceptors, which may have been launched on a track meant to hit a ballistic object. This pull-up may occur 100 or more kilometres from the surface target, if previous steerable re-entry vehicles are any indication,[16] but much depends on how well it is aimed.[17]

At some point after it slows down, the warhead's seeker will turn on. A radar, and perhaps other sensors, will sweep the sea in front of it, searching for a warship. If it finds what it is looking for, the RV will push itself onto a more precise trajectory that will carry it to a point almost directly above its target. Then it dives, a suicidal bird of prey, following sensor data in its final moments of flight as it tries to drive itself through the carrier's flight deck.

How Big a Bang?

What happens next is entirely speculative; nothing is publicly known about what sorts of fuzing the DF-21D has and whether it is meant to have any special effects on an aircraft carrier. The warhead's velocity will carry it through the flight deck's steel and into the compartments below. Despite its enormous speed, it is unlikely a DF-21D warhead could penetrate the two dozen or so levels of a carrier and put a hole in the bottom. There is simply too much reinforced metal and engineering meant to prevent such a fate. Instead, the warhead is more likely to detonate below deck, blasting the energy from 600kg of high explosives into ruptured

The USS *Theodore Roosevelt* (CVN-71) steams through the South China Sea, one of several supercarriers that regularly operate in the region. (US Navy)

compartments alongside the heat and fragments of the impact. Chinese state media is less circumspect, quoting officials as saying things like the DF-21D is 'capable of destroying an aircraft carrier with one hit.'[18]

Weapon effects on a modern supercarrier are, to some extent, state secrets. Indeed, the US Navy conducted the only modern study of anti-ship weapons on a supercarrier, the ex-USS *America* in 2005, out of view. Little has been made public about the findings, but the ship stayed afloat for weeks despite all the simulated battle damage and, in the end, had to be scuttled.[19] Depending on where an ASBM hits, the destruction could range from mild to catastrophic. Damaging a magazine or fuel store – buried deep below deck – is improbable but could create catastrophic explosions. Wrecking the ship's reactor would be little different from sinking it; destroying its elevators or catapults would be a mission kill. However, aircraft carriers are, after all, warships – they are built to survive a battle, and the crews train intensively on damage control.[20] In most scenarios, a single hit would not send a supercarrier to the bottom – but its fighting capabilities would be reduced, if only by virtue of being able to launch and recover fewer aircraft.[21]

Watchful Eyes

For that reason, and others related to ISR and sensors, any attack on a carrier strike group would involve several missiles – perhaps even dozens. The stakes of an out-and-out miss are high; the geopolitical dangers of a ballistic missile attack are considerable, as they can prod a conflict into much higher gear. For China, or any country wielding ASBMs, each shot needs to count.

Surveillance capability and solid targeting data, therefore, are perhaps just as important as the missiles themselves. China has developed an increasingly large range of radars on land, at sea and in the air, satellites, and undersea sensors to address this. Some of the advances have been technological; others are a matter of adding

platforms and basing. The man-made islands in the South China Sea, for example, allow Beijing to peer deeper into the waters it claims as its own than ever before.

The oldest and cheapest method of detecting fleets and their aircraft at long distances is massive land-based radar arrays. These systems, often the size of athletic fields and standing as tall as a modest skyscraper, bounce radio waves off the upper atmosphere back down to the surface, picking up the scattered returns and processing them into a picture of what objects might be out there. These over-the-horizon, or OTH, systems were developed during the Cold War as a means of early detection for bomber, missile and naval strikes; the technology is well understood and not all that expensive to deploy.[22]

China operates several of these,[23] and although it does not officially discuss them or disclose their locations, at least a few have been spotted on publicly available satellite images. The eastern coastal city of Wenzhou is home to a transmitter and receiver array, installed separately a few hundred meters apart. The coastal positioning – as opposed to in the north, where an over-the-pole missile attack would first appear – and the existence of such radars in China's South China Sea installations implies these systems are meant for maritime surveillance.[24]

Their exact capabilities are not known; the smaller island-based systems are suspected to have an active detection range of 250km,[25] but large Western and Soviet systems, which are well documented, imply China's could have ranges of several thousand kilometres. US OTH systems have been used for drug interdiction missions, which suggests a resolution much smaller than what would be needed to spot a warship.[26]

The main drawback of OTH radar is a lack of precision. It can tell an operator that there is a vessel somewhere in a ballpark that is hundreds of square kilometres in area, or more. This is not a huge issue when such radars task aircraft in friendly skies to search for

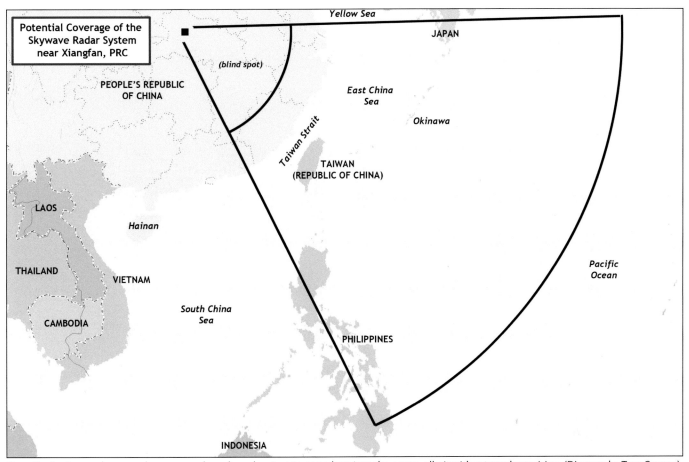

Over-the-horizon radar uses a long-range shore-based system to peer deep into the ocean, albeit without much precision. (Diagram by Tom Cooper)

smugglers or illegal fishing. But it is more significant when trying to aim a missile at a defended, manoeuvring target thousands of kilometres away. Indeed, the radars may even out-range the DF-21D (but not the longer-legged DF-26), making them more useful for aiming more precise sensors at a swath of sea than for providing targeting coordinates to a missile battery.

Sea- and air-based radars, on the other hand, can nail down the exact location of a ship. China operates the Type 346 phased array radar at sea, playing roughly same role as the US Navy's SPY-1 systems.[27] In the air, its surveillance and AWACS aircraft use radars about which little is publicly known; the most advanced, such as the KJ-2000 and KJ-500, are thought to use advanced active electronically scanned arrays.[28] (Its latest AWACS plane, the carrier-capable KJ-600, was still undergoing test flights in early 2021.[29]) As with the ground-based systems, their exact capabilities are not public, or at least widely discussed. But published reports suggest that the sea-based radars can spot surface targets as far out as several hundred kilometres,

China's Type 346 (NATO reporting name Dragon Eye) radar, a rough analogue to the US military's Aegis system, can spot surface targets more than 100 kilometres away. (US Navy)

The Y-8 maritime patrol aircraft, loosely based on the Antonov A-12, can hunt for American submarines in the South China Sea from bases in the Spratlys. (eng.chinamil.com.cn/)

and can operate passively, listening for emissions that would give away a ship's position. In the air, its modern AWACS variants can spot enemy targets up to 470 kilometres away.[30] However, Western systems like the SPY-1 and SPY-6 would most likely pick up active searches, providing a warning, if not a vector for attacking the ships or aircraft hunting for a carrier. Although the People's Liberation Army Navy flies aircraft, including drones,[31] with sensitive cameras and optical sensors, placing flying them within visual range of an enemy warship is inviting a surface-to-air missile, laser or airborne interception. They are a dubious choice for ASBM targeting.

The People's Liberation Army has also placed undersea sensors – mostly likely acoustic, listening for the sounds of ships and other enemy activity – around the South China Sea.[32] Like the OTH radar systems, on their own they cannot provide the sort of precision needed to launch a ballistic missile at a moving ship. But they can narrow a search area for other, more precise sensors, and provide

other important data such as speed and heading.[33] At least two such sensor networks are publicly known, both in the deepest parts of the Pacific Ocean, including the Challenger Deep.[34] Beijing says they are for scientific research, and indeed, passive undersea listening devices can sense heavy weather, earthquakes and even large aquatic life like whales. But they can also, for instance, monitor the comings and goings of ships from Guam and Yokosuka, Japan. And their location – literal miles undersea – makes it difficult to tamper with them or disable them.

Satellites give China the best overview of the waters it wishes to control. It has launched dozens of observation birds in the last two decades, some of which are military or dual-purpose. Beijing holds their precise capabilities close to the vest, but many of their orbits have been plotted; amateur observers estimate that a Chinese satellite passes over the South China Sea 20 to 50 times a day.[35] Optical satellites would have no problem spotting something the size

China's six Type 52C (Luyang II) destroyers carry the powerful Type 346 Dragon Eye radar, as well as anti-ship weapons. (US Department of Defense)

of an aircraft carrier (even commercial satellites, with a resolution ranging from 30cm to 1 meter – meaning that is the minimum size object they can see from orbit – could do it), but radar, which is unbothered by clouds or other atmospheric effects, would be a better pick for the job.[36]

China's bases in the Spratlys and other man-made islands also leave it well positioned to just listen for US warships. Under most circumstances, a fleet must communicate with its components and with command centres back on land. Each broadcast is an opportunity for eavesdropping. Picking up and analysing enemy communications, called signals intelligence or SIGINT, is another way the People's Liberation Army could zero in on a US fleet.

Ready, Aim …

But once data about fleet locations, sizes and headings start rolling in, it is up to analysts to figure out what to make of it all. As noted, some sensors provide a picture that is more of a sketch than a photograph. Satellites, on the other hand, offer pinpoint locations but can require hours to move into position.[37] Weaving all that information together takes work, experience and, perhaps most important for the purposes of attacking an enemy fleet, time.

Targeting analysis is a laborious process even for a stationary target, and the complications only multiply if the quarry is on the move – particularly in a congested environment like global maritime transit lanes. China's targeting doctrine is, as with many aspects of its military operations, opaque. In the US, the process begins with a commander providing guidance: making clear the intention to strike certain targets or achieve certain goals, often via written order. Targeteers will then do 'target development', analysing where the intended target is and what effects need to be achieved against it (for instance, an air defence site might be neutralized if the radar is destroyed, meaning other support equipment need not be attacked). Once that is determined, a particular munition is recommended for the target. For China, the target would be a ship, and its range from the mainland may put it out of range of aircraft or cruise missiles. That leaves only ASBMs to get the job done. The intelligence cycle spins alongside the targeting process. Commanders provide tasking, assets are assigned to collect data or imagery, and analysts comb through the results looking for their intended targets. Combat forces use the finished analytic products and provide feedback on their usefulness and effectiveness.

Leading up to a fight, the early stages like target development and weapon choice can be prepped; one assumes China is doing so right now with respect to US ships and bases within reach of its missiles. But in combat, all the analysis takes a non-trivial amount of time, adding further complexity to the task as the target ship continues to move, and possibly change course.

Once analysts have synthesized a clear picture of where the enemy fleet is, mission planners must decide how to use that information. The position information will be saddled with a confidence

rating or a probability percentage; for instance, planners might be told that there is a 50 percent chance the target is in a circle 20 kilometres in diameter, or a 100 percent chance it is in a circle 50 kilometres in diameter. The bigger the area where the target might be, the more missiles must be tasked to attacking it, with the knowledge that some will hit water and not steel.[38]

Planners must also account for enemy countermeasures. The US Navy has invested billions in its Aegis combat systems, which in recent years have been upgraded to engage ballistic missiles, including the purpose-built SM-3. Each DF-21D or other ASBM will most likely be equipped with decoys such as balloons or other debris that will fly alongside the missile in space, giving midcourse interceptors a more confusing and cluttered picture of what to attack. AN/SPY-1, and the SM-3's onboard sensors, are designed to sort out what is a target and what is not. There is no clear indication of who has the upper hand in this scenario, but it is vanishingly improbable that all the ASBMs that leave their launch vehicles will make it to their targets. Inevitable technical failures will further reduce the number of missiles that get through; the well-tested and much-used Tomahawk cruise missile, for instance, had at least one failure or 'clobber' in attacks against targets in Syria in 2017 and 2018.[39]

The missile costs and escalatory risks of an ASBM attack means they probably will be used only against high-value targets like aircraft carriers, and not just 'to take out anything that floats.'[40] A single target, surrounded by a defensive picket, in a vast ocean could require dozens of DF-21Ds to get through, let alone guarantee a sinking or mission kill. Using up a big enough chunk of China's ASBM inventory[41] limits its ability for a follow-up attack and underscoring the importance and difficulty of planning such a strike.

… Fire

Whatever recommendation is made, there is a good chance it must be approved at the highest levels of the Chinese Communist Party – at least at the start of a war. This reflects a key element of the DF-21D's function, by virtue of its position in the People's Liberation Army Rocket Force, which also controls China's strategic arsenal.[42] Both it and the DF-26 can be fitted with nuclear warheads, and given the additional escalatory risks of attacking the beating heart of the US fleet is almost certain to require sign-off for launch: 'The Chinese military does not delegate.'[43]

China's military drills constantly for scenarios like the invasion of Taiwan, which would require near-total sea control. (US Department of Defense)

A formation of Dong Feng-26 conventional and nuclear missiles takes part in a military parade during the celebrations marking the 70th anniversary of the founding of the People's Republic of China in 2019. (eng.chinamil.com.cn)

When that sign-off comes, it will be sent down to PLARF commanders, who will relay it to DF-21D brigades,[44] who will program and launch their weapons, aiming at a target they cannot see with missiles whose effects they will not witness. Because the DF-21D and DF-26 are solid-fuelled, launch preparations will take minutes instead of hours. After launch, the transporter-erector-launchers, or TELs, will move to a new location for rearming and refuelling, and to avoid a counterstrike.

The first phase of the missile's flight is, countermeasures aside, its most fraught; propulsion issues are by far the most common cause of rocket failures.[45] The forces of acceleration and the drag of the atmosphere are higher than they will be at any other point, and its guidance hardware is fighting to get the missile pointed in the right direction. Systems, including engines, are most likely to fail at this point, and some of the DF-21Ds in a large salvo may not make it into space. For reference, about 7 percent of the Minuteman III's 200-plus test flights have failed.[46]

Once the missile's first stage burns out, life gets easier for the DF-21D. A smaller second-stage motor pushes it above the atmosphere sends it coasting toward its target.[47] Soon after reaching space, the second stage separates from the warhead. Advanced missile designs often release countermeasures at this point, including bits and pieces of airframe, engines or fuel tanks, meant to confuse incoming interceptors. It may also deploy purpose-built decoys meant to mimic the radar return, appearance and even infrared signature of a warhead.[48] The re-entry vehicle cannot manoeuvre outside the atmosphere, following a trajectory defined by velocity and gravity; its return to the atmosphere is an inevitability rather than a choice. This is the stage of flight in which

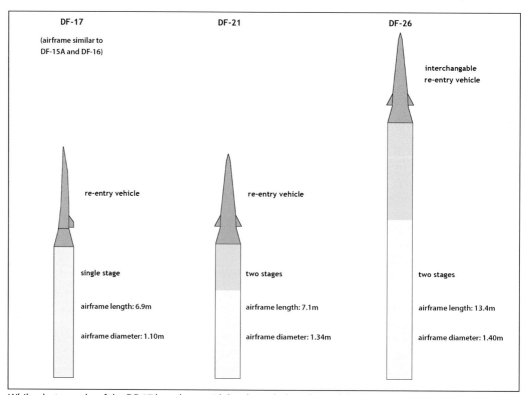

While photographs of the DF-17 have been widely released, clear shots of the DF-21, its -21D variant, and the DF-26 are rarely captured with sufficient fidelity for a side-by-side comparison. Thus, this depiction relies upon those rare images as well as images of their older 'cousins' to approximate the missiles themselves. (Diagram by Tom Cooper)

it is most vulnerable to direct attack.[49] Although it is screaming through space at many times the velocity of a bullet, its path is known and unchanging. If an interceptor can ignore the decoys and other countermeasures it can strike and destroy the warhead.

The terminal phase, when an ASBM warhead re-enters the atmosphere, is when the magic happens. Some sources have suggested the DF-21D receives outside targeting data in its midcourse or terminal phases of flight.[50] But in any event, its preprogramed targeting coordinates will give it a general area to examine, and some Chinese sources have suggested that it has a cross-range ability of up to 100km, meaning it can turn and hit a target 50km to the relative left or right of its original aimpoint.

The End of the Road
Re-entry vehicles do not contain systems for defeating missiles or dodging bullets. But an ASBM's high speed and ability to manoeuvre gives it an advantage against them. Because it relies on terminal guidance, it is more vulnerable to jamming, spoofing or blinding than ordinary re-entry vehicles. Even if a DF-21D warhead is flying blind, however, it still has the last known position of its target, or at worst its original aimpoint, giving it a puncher's chance of scoring a hit. If the re-entry vehicle is networked with its peers – a speculative but possible capability – it could even steer itself using information from other functioning warheads.

After all the warheads have ended their journey, encountering saltwater or a deck, both sides will take stock of their effects. It is likely that Western counterattacks are already under way; the degree of damage suffered is less important in that regard than the fact that an attack took place. But if a carrier has been sent to the bottom, along with its thousands of crew and billions of dollars' worth of aircraft, the retaliation will be more severe.[51] Data surrounding the attack, including radar tracks, re-entry vehicle behaviour and the effectiveness of countermeasures, will be pouring in for analysis. On the Chinese side, planners and politicians will be eager to see how well their weapons fared in their first combat use. With many variables now filled in, the high-risk, high-reward calculus

of attacking a carrier strike group with ballistic missiles could be evaluated.

The technology inside the DF-21D is not new or novel or even, by the standards of other cutting-edge weapons, all that complex. The individual processes that guide its flight are not either. Fitting them all together is the tough part, but even that does not present any impossibilities for an attacker.

The DF-21D flies as other missiles do, obeys the same laws of physics and leans on subsystems that are in wide use elsewhere. Some of the processes it uses to strike a moving target at sea are the same, or nearly the same, as those used decades earlier to guide ballistic missiles toward targets on land and sea. That does not mean that coaxing it to perform as advertised would be easy. The distances and countermeasures involved can make planning and executing an ASBM strike harder than using more conventional anti-ship weapons, albeit at much longer ranges. Each point of failure represents a link in a lengthy kill chain.

The kill chain is of course not a matter of technology inside the missile – but it is a crucial part of how an ASBM works. Aiming at a distant point is hard; finding a moving target among millions of square kilometres of ocean is harder. Massaging all the available data into a missile aimpoint is harder still. And the time needed to formulate a plan, calculate geopolitical risks, get permission to launch, and execute the attack make the DF-21D's mission a tricky proposition relative to striking a fixed target on land.

The DF-21D iterates on generations of missile designs, and as a result, many of the technical barriers for the weapon itself have already been ripped down. The environment it operates in, however, is far more hostile than at any point in history. A wicked array of countermeasures, including interceptor missiles that can strike a target in space and murder it with pure kinetic energy, now stands between an ASBM and its potential prey. Whether the DF-21D can overcome those, and connect the many dots of its kill chain, remains an open question until it is tested in a contested environment or used in war.

4
THREAT OR THEATER?

From the moment the DF-21D arrived on the scene, rumbling through a National Day parade in 2015, one question has lingered around it like a launch plume: does it work?

The fearsome possibilities of a weapon that can strike ships thousands of kilometres away are hard to overstate. At little immediate risk to its own units, an attacker could inflict massive damage on an expensive, difficult-to-replace fleet and relax the enemy's control of the sea for its own operations. For China, whose regional ambitions include establishing ownership of the South China Sea, such long-range dominance of the waves is an attractive proposition.[1]

China's state media has sounded a steady drumbeat of warnings that the DF-21D can sweep enemy carriers off the board, quoting ministers, military personnel and others as they repeat variations of 'China has the capability to make the US lose its aircraft carriers.'[2]

Yet for more than a decade, the system went untested against a realistic target – or even one floating motionless at sea. Although

Beijing has used state media to frame anti-ship ballistic missiles as a technology only China had the ability to produce,[3] the principles behind a manoeuvring warhead are not novel or new from an engineering perspective. Steering vanes that can drastically alter the trajectories of a warhead have appeared on operational designs dating back to the 1960s.

The Pershing II MRBM, of which the United States deployed hundreds starting in 1983,[4] pulled up 100 or more kilometres' from its target and 'glided,' nearly horizontally, until it was over the target, at which point it dived vertically and hit an aimpoint with a theoretical minimum size of about 30 meters. The pull-up phase allowed cross-range manoeuvring, but it was estimated to be 'too inaccurate, by a factor of five or ten, for the delivery of conventional warheads.'[5] The Soviets' R-27K was accurate enough to kill ships with nuclear warheads, but finding those ships in the first place was too difficult, and the project was abandoned.

In both cases, the technology of a steerable re-entry vehicle was simple: Radar or enemy emissions guided the warheads to their targets, much as they do on other weapons like cruise missiles. If the radar failed, inertial guidance took over.[6] (Ordinary ballistic missiles, such as the Minuteman III ICBM, follow a predictable path after booster burnout, determined by nothing more than classical mechanics.) ASBMs like the DF-21D work much as the Pershing II and R-27K did, moving in three dimensions to both confuse defences and take careful aim at their target.[7]

But using a conventional warhead to attack a moving target far from friendly units poses an intelligence, surveillance and reconnaissance problem that is onerous even for more traditional weapons like Russia's nascent Zircon high-speed cruise missile.[8]

Show Me

An end-to-end demonstration of the DF-21D has thus been seen as crucial to setting up China's ASBM arsenal as the game-changer Beijing would like it to be. The first suspected test came in 2007, revealed when satellite images found in 2013 showed shapes in the Gobi Desert that resembled the top-down footprint of a supercarrier.[9] Other pictures emerged of separate test areas showing the clear outlines of US Navy warships clustered together in a way that suggested they were moored in port.[10]

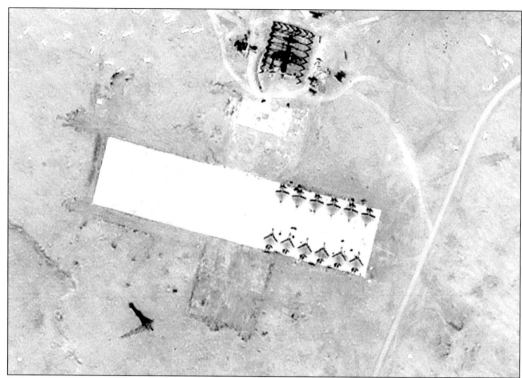

A target on the outer edge of China's Gobi Desert, seen here in 2013, was arranged to look like an aircraft carrier's deck and targeted with ballistic missiles. (Image copyright 2020 Maxar Technologies)

Another remote target deep inside China shows missile impact craters in 2007. The target area is roughly the size of a supercarrier flight deck. (Image copyright 2020 Maxar Technologies)

Also clear were the dozens of craters clustered on the 'decks' of the targets. Whatever punch the warheads delivered, and whatever real-world damage it may have done to an actual ship, they hit what they were meant to hit. The images showed that the DF-21D was capable of tremendous accuracy against a stationary target – although it was not clear that such accuracy was the result of terminal guidance.

That setup offered little insight into the key capabilities that would make a 'carrier killer' live up to its name. Hitting a ship at anchor is not much different from hitting an aircraft hangar or runway, which is a capability most modern militaries – including China's – have had for some time, in the form of ballistic missiles and cruise missiles. Although being able to drop devastation from space onto enemy installations is a serious threat on its own, it poses minimal risk to an adversary after it leaves the harbour.

In 2019, tests moved farther into the real world as DF-21Ds were fired from the mainland into the sea as far as 1,000 kilometres offshore. There was no direct reporting of the test's objectives and whether they were met. But China closed the intended target areas to air and marine traffic days in advance,[11] and the shots may have been tracked by foreign radars. This did not establish much more about whether the DF-21D could do what it says on the box, but it did show China did, at the very least, have the missile range to make carrier captains sweat.

The biggest step came in 2020, when word began to circulate that China had tested ASBMs against a moving target at sea. That was seemingly confirmed in November 2020, when US Navy Admiral

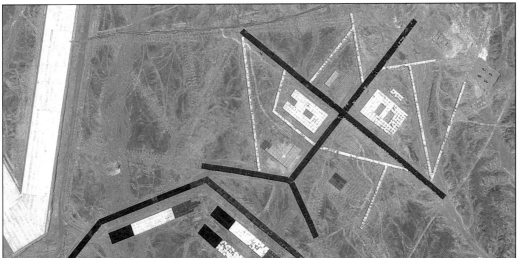

An elaborate mock-up of a naval base, including several ship-shaped targets, was built and targeted with ballistic missile tests in the Gobi Desert in China. (Image copyright 2020 Maxar Technologies)

Even Davidson chose his words carefully, declining to say that the missiles had struck their marks: 'They did test an anti-ship ballistic missile against a moving target. I'll leave it at that.'[15] Months later, Vice Admiral Jeffrey Trussler, the deputy chief of naval operations for information warfare, implied that the US Navy was unimpressed with the performance of China's ASBMs.[16]

In 2021, another wrinkle emerged: after testing at sea, China moved ASBM development back on land in the Taklamakan Desert. New facilities included two Arleigh Burke-shaped targets, and one target in the shape of a US supercarrier. On top of that, there was a warship-sized model mounted on 6-meter-wide tracks that appeared to be designed to carry it on an S-shaped path for several kilometers. One possible implication is that they were unsatisfied with the missile's performance in its closest approach to a real-world test. "They are still far from creating an accurate ASBM," said Collin Koh, a research fellow at the S. Rajaratnam School of International Studies in Singapore. "I don't think the desert targets are going to be the final stage. It's meant for further refinement."[17]

Philip Davidson, who led Indo-Pacific Command, said the test had involved launching one DF-21D and one DF-26 in an ASBM configuration at a moving vessel. It marked the first known time China had attempted the feat. To many, including Davidson, it came as no surprise: 'We've known for years that they were in pursuit of a capability that could attack moving targets.'[12]

However, there was no explicit confirmation from the Chinese government, military or state media that the warheads hit their targets – although the tests were described as 'successful.'[13] Allowing ambiguity about whether a high-profile weapon works is unusual for China's military. The People's Liberation Army is not shy about publicizing footage of successful surface-to-air missile tests and drills, and the People's Liberation Army Air Force regularly posts videos of its aircraft and pilots, sometimes dressing up the footage with Hollywood-style CGI effects. Military-linked publications in China often include updates on cutting-edge weapons such as rail guns, new aircraft carriers and stealth aircraft.[14]

So the DF-21D, even now, remains shrouded in a haze of incomplete information. Some analysts suggest the opacity may be deliberate and is meant to create a greater sense of alarm and deterrence. A more sceptical view might be that if China could demonstrate a hit against a moving target at sea, it would have done so—and that the fact it has not indicates a lack of confidence in the system.[18] But even without definitive proof that the missile and its

J-15 strike fighters are China's only operational carrier-based aircraft, based on the successful Russian-made Su-27. ((Ministry of National Defence PRC))

predecessor work as advertised, there is zero chance any military would assume it did not, and ignore the potential threat of such a capability.[19]

A Many-Splendored Missile

Even if the missiles cannot engage moving targets at sea, even if they are just suggestively named weapons with no exotic capabilities, they are still valuable. The precision of a manoeuvrable re-entry vehicle is useful for attacking high-value enemy facilities around Asia. There is no, or very little, opportunity cost to having hundreds of intermediate-range ballistic missiles that cannot kill ships but can kill lots of other stuff.[20] Indeed, the DF-26 is ostensibly a 'normal' ballistic missile but can carry an ASBM warhead. Most of the DF-26 inventory is tasked with attacking targets on land.[21]

To some degree, this dual capability of China's ASBMs is their biggest threat to Western militaries: a good way to keep a fleet at arm's length is to make sure it never leaves the harbour, or has no ports available. For a country like the United States, which would fight a naval war with China thousands of miles from American shores, damaged or destroyed facilities in Japan and Guam, for instance, would make a prolonged fight much more difficult. A sneak attack, catching key ships and materiel in port could be even more devastating.

This scenario is seen as one of the most alarming for the US Navy, which, with the addition of a possible 1st Fleet to go with the 7th Fleet already operating in and around China, needs all the facilities it can get.[22] The addition of Aegis Ashore batteries in Japan, and stationing Aegis ships and THAAD batteries in Guam, mitigates but does not eliminate the threat.[23] Planners try to ensure most of the fleet is at sea in the Indo-Pacific region at any one time, but that

operational tempo grinds down morale and personnel, as the USS *Fitzgerald* and USS *McCain* incidents attest.[24] The US military's fallback plan if it loses its bases in Japan and Guam is to disperse operations elsewhere in the region, to places such as Australia or even the Philippines.[25] Of course, if facilities in Japan are destroyed, a regional war is already well under way and most plans are many iterations into their contingencies.

China's ASBMs pose a grave danger to the US military's stationary targets. In that sense, the answer to the question, 'do China's ASBMs work?' is an unequivocal yes.

Using an ASBM-compatible weapon against a land target is not risk-free, however. Any attack carries the near-certainty of retaliation – but using long-range ballistic missiles piles on the danger. No country has ever launched a large-scale ballistic missile attack at the sorts of ranges needed to hit a fleet at sea or targets as distant as Guam. Such an attack raises the so-called discrimination problem, when an adversary has just a few minutes to determine whether there is a flight of nuclear-armed missiles inbound, or 'just' conventional warheads.[26] The difference between the two, of course, is the difference between a massive conventional retaliation and the first use of nuclear weapons in anger since 1945.

China has a no-first-use policy for nuclear weapons, however, and no ability to destroy the US nuclear arsenal to prevent a counterstrike. Even so, it is not altogether clear how the US military, and its civilian leaders, would respond to even a conventional massed ballistic missile attack against targets outside the United States. Retaliation is assured, but what to hit – and how hard – is murky, as is whether the implied threat of such a counterpunch would be enough to deter a missile attack in the first place. Some say even an otherwise catastrophic outcome for the PRC would be

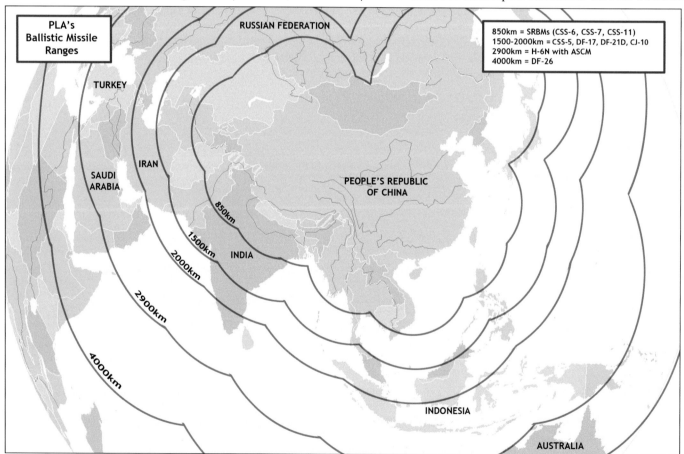

China's older, short-range ballistic missiles (SRBMs), air-launched cruise missiles (ALCMs), air-launched versions of the DF-21, and its surface-launched DF-21D and DF-26 missiles can reach far away from China and well into the Pacific Ocean, thus representing an early threat to any approaching naval force. (Map by Tom Cooper)

The Royal Australian Navy guided-missile destroyer HMAS *Brisbane* (DDG 41), Japanese Maritime Self-Defense Force destroyer JS *Makinami* (DD 112), Republic of Korea Navy destroyer ROKS *Wang Geon* (DDH 978), and US Navy guided-missile destroyer USS *Rafael Peralta* (DDG-115) sail through the Tasman Sea. Such vessels, operated by the United States and its allies, are seen as crucial to keeping the South China Sea open during a conflict. (Royal Australian Navy)

Wasp-class amphibious assault ships such as the USS *Makin Island* (LHD-8) are another way the US Navy can project power at sea. They carry fewer strike aircraft than a supercarrier but have the firepower for an amphibious landing. (US Navy)

acceptable in exchange for a prize like Taiwan. 'How do you issue a credible threat of a painful enough response that China wouldn't consider using these extremely effective weapons? If you say to Xi Jinping, 'You lose your whole navy but you get Taiwan,' he may well say, 'Fine—I'll take Taiwan. I can rebuild my navy.'[27]

Countless hours of simulations and planning during the Cold War sought to assess what an intercontinental ballistic missile attack would look like and how much time there would be to respond. Ready-to-go counterattack plans gave leaders a menu of responses to make the decision easier, or at least faster. Such plans are secret. The exact shape of a Western response to a Chinese ballistic missile attack remains unknown, and as Sun Tzu wrote, 'Everyone has a plan until they get punched in the mouth.'[28] Both sides are wary of a conflict escalating out of control before, and perhaps exclusive to, any strategic goals being accomplished. Those factors may limit the battlefield use of the DF-21D and DF-26 as anything but weapons of desperation or as the leading edge of a first strike that kicks off a major conflagration.

Playing Defence

One of the ways ASBMs could alter the calculus of battle – even if one never takes flight – is to force Western navies to change the types of defensive missiles they carry, and perhaps even eliminate offensive firepower in favour of munitions meant to knock ballistic missiles out of the sky.

The exact mix of missiles US cruisers and destroyers carry is classified; typically, it is some combination of BGM-109 Tomahawks and Standard Missiles (SM-3 and SM-6).[29] For decades, the Navy's defensive armament was devoted to slapping down cruise missiles or knocking enemy aircraft out of the sky. The addition of an anti-ballistic missile mission put more SM-3 rounds onboard – an important change, because these interceptors cannot engage targets in the atmosphere. If the ships themselves are now targets for ballistic missiles, more SM-3 rounds will be needed, complicating air defence. The advent of the SM-6,[30] which can operate in the atmosphere and engage ballistic missiles in their terminal phase, helps with this conundrum. But it is not a silver bullet, as point defence against a ballistic missile is much harder – and less likely to succeed – than attacking it in space.

China has a toothy array of other anti-ship weapons, including hundreds of anti-ship missiles such as the YJ-12 family, which has a range of 300 kilometres and is known to be based on mainland shores, at sea and on the manmade islands in the South China Sea.[31] The People's Liberation Army Navy also has 52 attack submarines, 46

An EA-18G Growler attached to the "Shadowhawks" of Electronic Attack Squadron 141 launches from the flight deck of the USS *Ronald Reagan*. The EA-18 is a crucial part of fleet defense, providing both detection and electronic warfare capabilities. (US Navy)

The MH-60R Sea Hawk helicopter is a key part of a carrier strike group's defenses against submarine surveillance and attack. (US Navy)

of which are diesel boats.[32] The less-advanced Chinese submarines may be taken off the board on Day One of a war, or they may survive long enough to attack a carrier strike group. But anti-submarine warfare is on the minds of any US Navy planner.[33]

Then there are air-launched missiles, lobbed from medium bombers or ship-launched aircraft.[34] Doctrinally, this sort of attack is not much different from the waves of cruise missiles with which the Soviet Union planned to darken the skies over the North Atlantic.[35] And China's lack of a modern heavy bomber fleet is mitigated by high-tech cruise missiles; 'these days, you don't really need a sophisticated platform when you have advanced missiles.'[36]

All of which is to say, a tsunami of weapons would be bearing down on US carrier strike groups if a war erupted with China – not just ASBMs. But adding the dimension of ballistic missiles to fleet defence means adding weapons, and ships to carry them, at

the expense of other systems. For a navy that is already stretched thin in both ships and personnel, that is a vexing problem.[37] In other words, China's opportunity cost for deploying ASBMs that can be used against land targets is nil. But every Tomahawk swapped out in favour of an air defence missile, and destroyer pulled into service in Asia, limits the United States' options in the South China Sea or elsewhere.

The ASBM threat in the South China Sea will not change the US Navy's day-to-day operations or keep it from places it wants to be in peacetime, as evidenced by regular Taiwan Strait transits.[38] But Chinese planners hope fears about the missile's capabilities make Western strategists hesitate to sail fleets within range of the DF-21D and DF-26 during a conflict.[39] This slight hesitation could be an advantage for China in the nascent stages of a big war.

The guided-missile cruiser USS *Princeton* (CG-59) and the guided-missile destroyer USS *Russell* (DDG-59) steam alongside the aircraft carrier USS *Nimitz* (CVN-68) in the Indo-Pacfic region. (US Navy)

Even the way a carrier strike group is physically organized on the ocean changes with the threat of a ballistic missile attack. Hitting a ballistic missile in flight is more than having interceptors in the air that can pull off the 'hit a bullet with a bullet' trick. The placement of sensors is crucial, as detecting an incoming ballistic missile (or even being alerted to its launch and early trajectory) can be the difference between a difficult shootdown and a nearly impossible one. Missile pickets, and their powerful radars, must be placed in a way that puts them between the theoretical ballistic threats and the aircraft carrier.[40] That means an unbalanced defence skewed toward platforms or more ships to defend the same area of sea.

All of which are more ways in which the DF-21D and its brethren 'work,' even if they stay nestled in their launchers.

Scoring a Bullseye

Hitting a moving ship is the toughest weapon effect for these missiles to achieve. It represents only the last moments of a process involving scores of people, multiple systems and command and control structures untested in wartime. These elements – in which the target must be spotted, the information transmitted to analysts, the analysts' views presented to decision makers, and the decisionmakers' order to fire transmitted to the missile batteries – represent many places in which an attack might fail.

To begin with, although a fleet is composed of millions of tons of steel and radar-reflective angles, doctrine has evolved over decades to disperse the fleet in ways that make a carrier difficult to track, or at least easily engage. The ships, including the outer defensive ring, can sail quietly, with sensors 'listening' for enemy activity rather

The E-2C Hawkeye, such as this one assigned to the "Liberty Bells" of Airborne Command and Control Squadron 115, provide early warning capability to carrier strike groups. (US Navy)

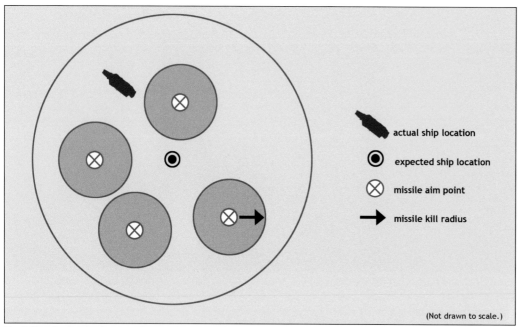

◣	actual ship location
◉	expected ship location
⊗	missile aim point
→	missile kill radius

(Not drawn to scale.)

The 'kill radius' is the distance from its aimpoint that an ASBM can be expected to acquire and hit a target. The 'targeting location error' is the distance from the expected target location that the target may actually be, because of movement and manoeuvring. (Diagram by Tom Cooper)

at an altitude of about 35,000 kilometres and can only fly above the Equator, giving them limited utility for this mission. Satellites that pass overhead every few hours work best but can only see a limited area for a limited time and must be aimed – or cued – if operators want to check a specific location. If a satellite is tasked with looking at the right place at the right time, its data would be available instantaneously, but objects of interest are more likely to be analysed and confirmed before being treated as actionable data.[46] Even if that only takes five or 10 minutes, a US warship would be kilometres from where it was spotted.

than actively searching for it, limiting stray radiation that could give away a fleet's position.[41]

The People's Liberation Army has poured money into high-powered radar systems and satellites over the last two decades.[42] The radars, based on shore, do not need to be passive; their general locations are known on the mainland and in the Spratly Islands,[43] and in the early days of a conflict they would be vulnerable. Their ranges and limitations are well understood, and planners can estimate courses that will make it harder for them to get a bead on an American fleet.[44] (See Chapter 3)

It is harder to hide from a satellite. Space-based radars (and cameras, although they are less useful because of clouds) can pick up something as huge as a warship, even in the vastness of the ocean; technologically, providing precise enough location data for a missile strike is not difficult.[45] Geostationary satellites, which can 'stare' from a fixed position relative to a spot on Earth, orbit

The targeting data must then make its way into the hands of commanders, running more time off the clock; before they can give the order to fire, they may need to get permission from the central government.[47] Their orders must be transmitted to ASBM batteries, which must then prepare to fire. Minutes after that, the missiles will be in the air. But each tick that passes complicates a successful attack.

One of the few reports to attempt to calculate the DF-21D's accuracy notes that as time passes, the imaginary circle in which a fleet could be after it was first spotted grows. The bigger that area becomes, the more missiles are required to create a decent probability of a hitting a carrier.[48] If the 'kill radius' of a DF-21D – the area of ocean in which it can see and steer itself to a target – is one-quarter the size of a theoretical circle that has a 50-50 chance of containing the target ship, the report estimates it would take 82 missiles to create an 80 percent chance of a kill, without countermeasures.[49] China fields only two brigades of DF-21Ds,

China will lean on its fleet of KJ-500 AEW&C aircraft during a conflict to spot incoming hostile forces and provide useful targeting data for its shore-based missiles. (eng.chinamil.com.cn/)

each with about a dozen launchers (although some sources have suggested a higher number).[50]

Targeting accuracy also determines how far the re-entry vehicle will need to 'fly' and thus slow down. A warhead that plunges out of space above a carrier will travel much faster than one that must zigzag in from hundreds of kilometres away, making it easier prey for a carrier strike group's missile defences.[51]

None of these issues face more conventional weapons such as cruise missiles, which are tasked using information from Earth- or air-based sensors, get in-flight updates and can use onboard instruments to adjust course as needed.[52]

The Chain Gang

Airborne sensors, such as aircraft equipped with powerful search radars, are a known part of the People's Liberation Army Air Force.[53] The KJ-500 AWACS aircraft[54] cannot operate from the country's rudimentary carriers, but several are based on its manmade islands in the South China Sea, and with an unrefuelled range of several thousand kilometres, they can stay in the air for hours. Such patrols were once a mainstay of anti-ship warfare, but as surface-to-air missiles developed longer legs, ISR aircraft are less likely to get within sensor range of an enemy fleet in the twenty-first century.

This part of the kill chain is vulnerable. US jammers can disrupt radars and slow communications. Satellites can be jammed, blinded, or destroyed.[55] Aircraft can be plucked from the sky with long-range missiles. And the farther from shore the target fleet is, the longer the kill chain becomes. The fact that Chinese state media has not been vociferous in portraying the success of the recent DF-21D and DF-26 tests against a moving target at sea may indicate a lack of confidence in how the kill chain will hold together in a contested environment. 'There is some recognition for exact conditions under which the missile is more or less effective.'[56] On the other hand, the US Navy can quickly move a half-dozen or so supercarriers and

amphibious assault ships, the types of vessels that ASBMs are meant to destroy, into Asia. China can only launch 24 DF-21Ds before rearming. That may imply Beijing is confident it needs just a few missiles aimed at each capital ship to get the job done.[57]

China's opaque command and control structure is a separate potential obstacle to a successful strike. The People's Liberation Army Rocket Force, or PLARF, is responsible for all the country's several thousand missiles, both nuclear and conventional.[58] Its ASBMs are not nuclear tipped. But the potential for swift escalation after attacking a high-value US unit means authorization for the PLARF to launch an ASBM attack on an American fleet would come from the upper echelons of Chinese Communist Party leadership. How fast can an analyst's data get to a commander, then to Xi Jinping, the de facto head of China's military? As noted, every minute of delay widens the theoretical circle where the target fleet might be.

This is a problem analysts have tried to game out regarding China's small but growing fleet of ballistic missile submarines, which are meant to carry a few dozen[59] of the country's 350 or so nuclear warheads. Staying hidden at sea means limiting, or eliminating, communication with the outside world. In other areas of China's military, doctrine puts few heavy decisions in the hands of field leaders. Would that be different for captains of ballistic missile submarines? Would they have the authority to launch without a direct order from Xi Jinping?[60] Answering those questions could offer insight into how the country would handle the launch of ASBMs.

Some literature speaks to an even more complex structure, in which launch authority rests not with the country's leader and Central Military Commission, but also in its Politburo, which must review any decision to use nuclear weapons. China's government is largely a rubber stamp for the policies of Xi Jinping, but the additional delay, no matter how small, in reviewing a decision may also add to the complexities of approving an ASBM attack. It also

The USS *Theodore Roosevelt* Carrier Strike Group steams in formation with the USS *Makin Island* Amphibious Ready Group in the South China Sea. (US Navy)

may add escalatory risk: 'It's the clearest possible signal that they are gunning for (America), that it is on.'[61]

Caution and layered decision-making do not seem unwarranted; again, the US could mistake a mass conventional ballistic missile attack for a nuclear strike, or even consider such an attack so escalatory and egregious as to warrant a nuclear response.[62] The odds seem slim that a battery commander could get targeting data for his DF-21Ds and make the decision on his own to let them fly unless a war was well under way and regular command channels degraded. That is not the case for China's anti-ship cruise missiles, which for reasons both practical and psychological are not as escalatory. That might make it more attractive for China to save its ASBMs for a last-ditch or desperation attack as opposed to the opening salvos of what is sure to be a bloody and savage conflict.

Deterrence, the Real MVP

The DF-21D, DF-26 and whatever missiles may come after them thus seem to represent less of a technological leap and more of a strategic shift. The engineering behind them has been around for decades. The guidance systems were honed and deployed in at least two weapons, the Pershing II and R-27K.

For all its ferocious talk and 'Wolf Warrior diplomacy,' China has a no-first-use policy and has shown no indication of being an irrational actor in terms of nuclear warfare.[63] Yet the escalatory risks of ASBMs have not deterred Beijing from ploughing resources into their development (the country does not publicly break down its defence spending by program[64]) and parading them in public. Their existence is a threat, an unsubtle message to the West[65] that the days of sailing a carrier strike group through the middle of a South China Sea conflict unchallenged, much less the Taiwan Strait, are over.

Their ability to strike a moving target at sea is asserted but not proven. No one has seen a ship with a smoking hole in the deck or watched electro-optical footage of an RV homing in on its target. And China's actions – from a lack of hype around a successful test, to the relatively small numbers of ASBMs, may tell a different story from the confident tones of state media.

The fact that there has been no evidence for further deployment since around 2012, and indeed some initial evidence to suggest both equipped brigades have already replaced their 21Ds with an unknown new missile system after less than a decade of service, it is possible that the 21D was more of a first-gen stab at

developing an effective ASBM, and probable that the PLARF has already shifted their resources to the next generation of ASBMs. We should gain greater clarity in the coming years by observing trends in how their ASBM force develops.[66]

Because DF-26s may be replacing DF-21Ds, it should be noted that even as more of the newer missiles enter service, it is not clear that the total number of China's ASBM warheads is increasing. If deployment stays steady at two brigades' worth, it is impossible to tell whether the Chinese military views them as a niche capability (and thus not worth buying a lot of) or a sure thing (meaning not many are needed to get the job done).

But to some degree, none of that is as important as the *theoretical* threat an ASBM poses to a ship. The risk to an American fleet may be low in absolute terms, but the potential devastation of a successful attack is so great that it moulds Western planning and doctrine. Fleets must plot courses to avoid as many of China's known sensors as possible; they must position warships to detect and intercept an incoming ballistic missile strike; they must change the mix of weapons they carry; they must add ships to deepen the fleet's magazines; they must develop new countermeasures. None are simple or come cheaply. China, by contrast, bears little extra cost, as its ASBMs can attack stationary targets as well as ships.

How, and whether, China uses these missiles is a thorny and enigmatic issue. Political control of China's ASBMs may complicate an attack's timing, and the escalatory risks of lobbing ballistic missiles at an enemy with the world's largest nuclear arsenal are considerable. The missiles may stay on the ground unless the situation is dire; sinking a carrier with a torpedo is just as devastating to the enemy and much less likely to provoke as ferocious a retaliation. And in any case, the kill chain is long and involves systems and processes that have never been tested together in a confrontational environment. That, complicated by Western countermeasures, represents the biggest obstacle to a DF-21D hitting its intended target.

Without a test that scores a hit against a moving target at sea, there is no proof for Beijing, or anyone else, that the DF-21D or DF-26 can send a carrier to the bottom. But the uncertainty may not matter. It has changed the calculus of seapower in a part of the world China wishes to bring under its control—and where Western navies have for more than 100 years operated with impunity. For now, China's ASBMs 'work,' even if they do not.

Two Chinese Jiangdao-class corvettes, Hanzhong (520) and Yongzhou (628) participating in a combat exercise in the South China Sea. (eng.chinamil.com.cn/)

A typical carrier air wing (CVW) of the US Navy, as of 2020–2022, consists of five squadrons equipped with sub-variants of the Boeing F/A-18 Super Hornet. As of late 2021, the first squadron of CVW-5, home-based in Japan, embarked aboard the USS *Ronald Reagan* (CVN-76) and underway in the south-western Pacific, were the Diamondbacks of VFA-102, operating two-seat F/A-18Fs. The example here is shown armed with AGM-158 JASSM GPS-guided, joint air-to-surface standoff missile, designed to provide a powerful edge in both strikes on ground and naval targets, through enabling the US Navy to attack targets from outside the range of enemy ground-based air defences. For self-defence, the aircraft can still be armed with AIM-120C AMRAAM and AIM-9X Sidewinder air-to-air missiles. (Artwork by Tom Cooper)

With the US Navy in the process of building up its fleet of Lockheed-Martin F-35C Lightning II stealth fighters, it rests upon single-seat F/A-18E Super Hornets to form the backbone of its fighter fleet. The second squadron of CVW-5 as of late 2021 was VFA-27, the Royal Maces. This Super Hornet from VFA-27 is shown armed for fleet defence with AIM-120C AMRAAM medium-range, active radar homing air-to-air missiles on underwing pylons, and AIM-9X Sidewinder short-range, infrared homing air-to-air missile on wingtip pylons. (Artwork by Tom Cooper)

The F/A-18E has a smaller radar cross section than the 'legacy' F/A-18A/B/C/D Hornets, allowing it to evade detection until closer to potential targets. This characteristic is likely to be very useful in an engagement with enemy warships. For such tasks, the US Navy still arms its Super Hornets with older anti-ship weapons, like the AGM-84 Harpoon. The latest Harpoon variant is here illustrated on an underwing pylon of a Super Hornet from the third squadron of CVW-5 as of late 2021 – the Eagles of VFA-115. The Harpoon is slower than the latest anti-ship missiles and carries a relatively small warhead, but it is still available in significant numbers: combined with its low cost, this results in it remaining a mainstay of the US Navy's anti-ship capability. (Artwork by Tom Cooper)

The fourth Super Hornet squadron of CVW-5, as of late 2021, was VFA-195, the Dambusters. This Super Hornet of that unit is shown armed with an AGM-84 SLAM standoff land attack missile. A further development of the old Harpoon, the SLAM is a subsonic, over-the-horizon cruise missile. It is equipped with a datalink connecting it to the launching aircraft, an inertial navigation system and GPS receiver for mid-course guidance, and a modified imaging-infrared seeker-head of the AGM-65F Maverick air-to-ground missile for the terminal flight phase, making it a highly precise weapon for standoff attacks on distant targets. From 2000, it was replaced by the AGM-84H SLAM-ER, which has numerous new capabilities, including improved target penetration and nearly twice the range of the original variant. (Artwork by Tom Cooper)

The fifth Super Hornet squadron of CVW-5, as of late 2021, was VAQ-141, the Shadowhawks. The Shadowhawks were equipped with the latest variant of this design, the EA-18G Growler, a specialised version designed for electronic warfare and equipped with modified ALQ-99 high- and low-band tactical jamming pods shown installed on underwing pylons. Thanks to its powerful electronic warfare system, the Growler would play a crucial role in any confrontation with China, when its task would be to disrupt parts of its kill chain and thus frustrate an ASBM attack by making the US fleet yet harder to find than it already is. (Artwork by Tom Cooper)

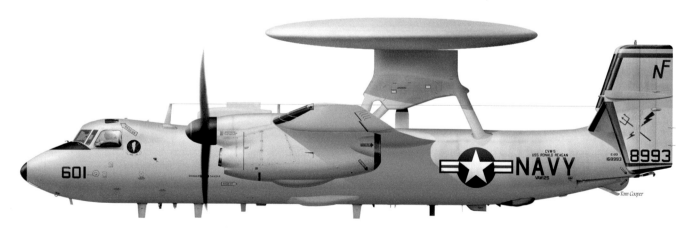

The sixth squadron of CVW-5 as of late 2021 was the Tigertails of VAW-125 (also known as 'Torch Bearers'), equipped with Northrop-Grumman E-2D Advanced Hawkeye early warning aircraft. In comparison to earlier versions of this type, the E-2D has an entirely new avionics suite, in-flight refuelling capability, and more powerful engines. Its AN/APX-9 radar is an active electronically scanned array, which adds electronic scanning to the mechanically rotated antenna inside the radome mounted above the fuselage. This system is suspected of being capable of detecting fighter-sized stealth aircraft (like the Chinese Chengdu J-20 and Shenyang J-31) from standoff ranges, and the capability to track ballistic missiles at least during their boost phase. The E-2D would be highly important for detecting enemy ISR platforms and thus forcing them to operate further away from the U.S. Navy's carriers, eliminating any capability to detect and track the movement of the ships it is protecting. (Artwork by Tom Cooper)

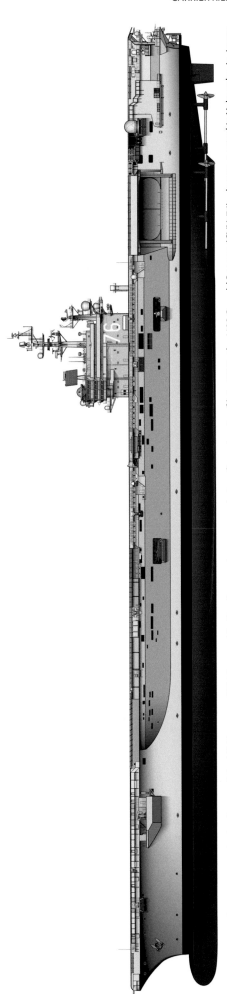

The centrepiece of every Carrier Strike Group of the US Navy as of 2022 was a Nimitz-class nuclear powered aircraft carrier. As of late 2021, the USS *Ronald Reagan* (CVN-76) – home-ported in Yokosuka, in Japan – served as the Navy's sole forward-deployed carrier and cruised the south-western pacific. About 332m (1,092ft) long, and displacing 101,400 long tons (113,600 short tons), *USS Ronald Reagan was* as long, but of slightly greater displacement than the USS *Nimitz* (CVN-68), which was also deployed in the South China Sea as of late 2021. Nick-named 'Gipper', USS *Ronald Reagan* is emblematic of the threat that Beijing set out to counter with its anti-ship ballistic missile program. (Artwork by Ivan Zajac)

Guided-missile cruisers of the Ticonderoga-class – like the Pearl Harbor-based USS *Lake Erie* (CG-70), illustrated here – form the nucleus of the carrier's defensive screen. Each packs two 61-cell Mk.41 vertical launch systems (VLS), usually containing a mix of RIM-66/156/161/162/174 Standard and ESSM air defence missiles, and Tomahawk cruise missiles. The Standard missile and ESSM are used in concert with the advanced version of the Aegis combat system, described as the most powerful air defence system in the world when entering service in the mid-1980s. The centrepiece of the Aegis is the AN/SPY-1A/B multi-function radar, which has four antennas covering the vessel. This system is capable of swatting down airborne threats and of launching offensive strikes at sea and against the shore. (Artwork by Ivan Zajac)

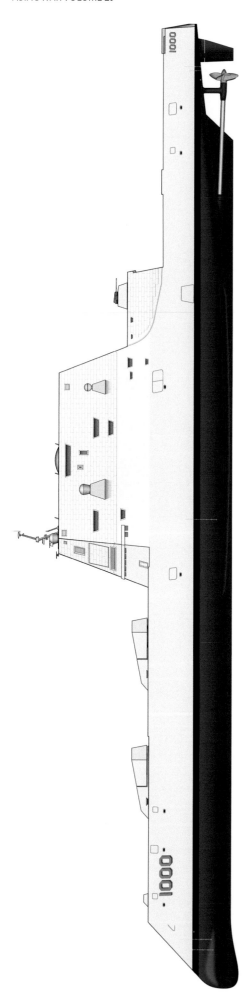

Zumwalt-class destroyers, like the USS *Zumwalt* (DDG-1000), shown here, were conceived as a combination of a stealth-formed, wave-piercing tumblehome hull packed with futuristic systems like railguns and directed-energy weapons. Originally intended as a 32-ship class, cost overruns and technology-related issues have reduced their procurement to only three cruiser-sized vessels (the others being USS *Michael Mansoor*, DDG-1001, and USS *Lyndon B Johnson*, DDG-1002). Their primary armament consists of 20 Mk.57 VLS modules, each with four cells, for a total of 80, filled with RIM-162 Evolved Sea Sparrow air defence missiles, Tomahawk cruise-missiles, and VLA anti-submarine missiles. (Artwork by Ivan Zajac)

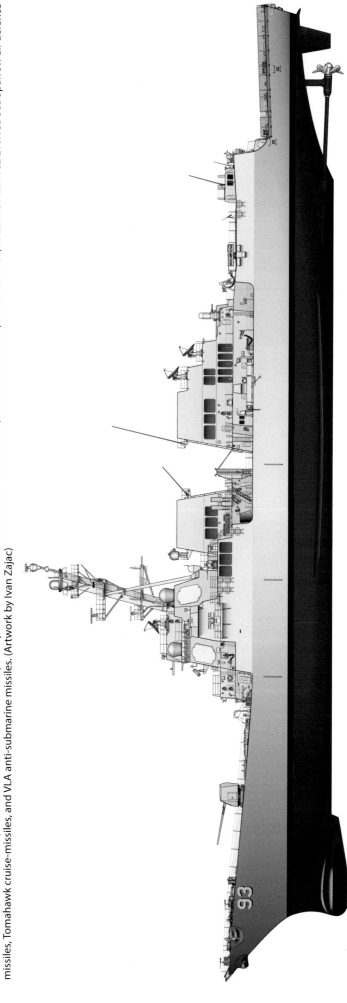

The workhorse of the US Navy as of the 2020 was the Arleigh Burke-class of guided-missile destroyers: a typical carrier strike group includes two or three such vessels – such as the USS *Chung Hoon* (DDG-93), shown here. Depending on the sub-variant, each carries 90–96 VLS cells, the Aegis combat system including the SPY-1 radar, and has extensive anti-submarine warfare capabilities. As such, they round out the defensive screen of every aircraft carrier, and pack both a considerable defensive and offensive punch. (Artwork by Ivan Zajac)

During the last decade, the People's Liberation Army Navy invested heavily in developing systems and building up a carrier fleet. Meanwhile, it operates two Type-001 aircraft carriers – *Liaoning* (hull number 16), and *Shandong* (hull number 17) – with a third, bigger, vessel under construction. The principal naval fighter aboard *Liaoning* and *Shandong* is the Shenyang J-15 Flying Shark (NATO-codename 'Flanker-X2'): a multi-role fighter derived from the Russian-made Sukhoi Su-27, equipped with air-to-air and anti-ship missiles. In the event of war, the J-15's main role would be to sweep the skies free of adversary aircraft. The example illustrated here – armed with PL-8 short-range and PL-12 medium range air-to-air missiles – belonged to the first batch of single-seaters, manufactured in the early 2010s. Shenyang is developing additional variants, including the J-15D, a two-seat electronic warfare aircraft. (Artwork by Tom Cooper)

Based on the airframe of the Shaanxi Y-9 transport (a further development of the Soviet-made Antonov An-12 design), the Shaanxi KJ-500 belongs to the third generation of Chinese-made airborne early warning and control aircraft. It is equipped with a radar using three active electronically scanned arrays installed in a fixed radome (to provide 360-degree coverage) and an informatised combat system enabling multi-functionality and networking of dozens of aircraft. While eight KJ-500s are operated by the PLAAF, including its 26th Special Mission Division, eight KJ-500Hs are in service with the PLANAF. (Artwork by Tom Cooper)

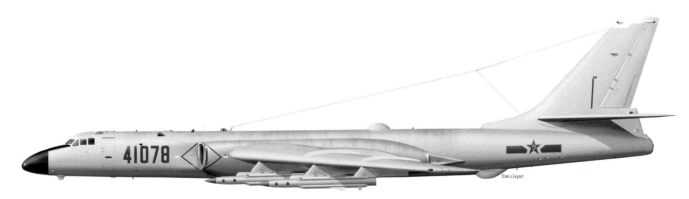

The latest member of the Xian H-6 bomber family (based on the Soviet-made Tupolev Tu-16 medium bomber) are the H-6K and H-6N versions, which feature a completely revised forward fuselage and (Russian-made) D-30KP-2 turbofan engines. Both can be equipped with an arsenal of up to six anti-ship and cruise missiles (such as YJ-12 supersonic anti-ship cruise missiles, illustrated here attached on underwing hardpoints). Moreover, the H-6N appears to be compatible with an air-launched variant of the DF-21 anti-ship ballistic missile, installed in a recess under the centre fuselage. Operated by the PLAAF, the primary role of H-6K/Ns is to hunt for surface vessels, creating an additional deadly problem for any potential adversary, including the US Navy. (Artwork by Tom Cooper)

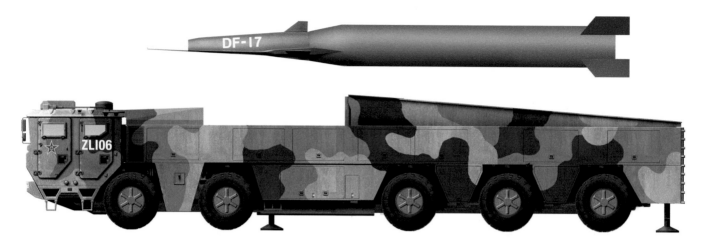

The DF-17's airplane-style shaping implies that it is designed for maneuverability – to make turns high in the atmosphere while traveling at high speeds. China has remained tight-lipped about what targets it is meant for, but has dropped hints it may eventually be able to engage ships. Because much of its flight to target occurs in the atmosphere, it must be engaged with an interceptor meant to function at such altitudes, such as the SM-6. (Artworks by David Bocquelet & Tom Cooper)

The WS2600 TEL for the DF-21 has five axles, giving it limited capability off paved roads. That offers the capability to rapidly disperse missiles before attacking from different directions, and provides flexibility in terms of where it can be reloaded. The DF-21D missile has never been publicly shown outside its launch container, but TELs camouflaged and marked this way have appeared in many parades and propaganda videos, building national pride and presenting evidence of their existance to the outside world. (Artwork by David Bocquelet)

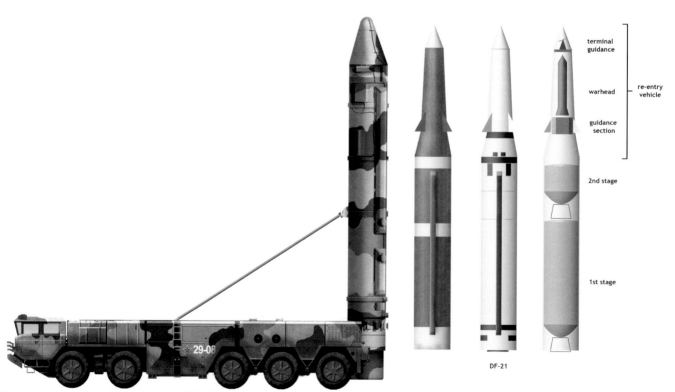

This is a reconstruction of an operational WS2600 TEL, with its launch container in erected position. Artworks to the right show an operational DF-21 missile (left), a test round (centre), and an approximate cross-section of the weapon, including its major parts. (Artworks by David Bocquelet & Tom Cooper)

Maneuvering warheads such as the one apparently displayed on the DF-17 offer several advantages. Not only can they complicate interceptions, they can conceal intentions: a missile that seems launched toward one target can change its course and engage a totally different one, or engage a single target from multiple directions. The more it maneuvers, however, the more it slows down–making it a potentially easier target for missile-defence systems. (Chinese Internet)

The DF-26, with a range of about 4,000 kilometers, holds US military assets at risk in a variety of ways. Its theoretical accuracy would allow it to strike facilities as far away as Guam with less than 30 minutes' notice, and potentially much less. The missiles can carry anti-ship warheads, pushing the threat to the US Navy much farther from China's shores. And perhaps most dangerous, they can be fitted with nuclear warheads in the field, making it all but impossible for adversaries to determine whether they are facing a strategic attack or a conventional one. (Chinese Internet)

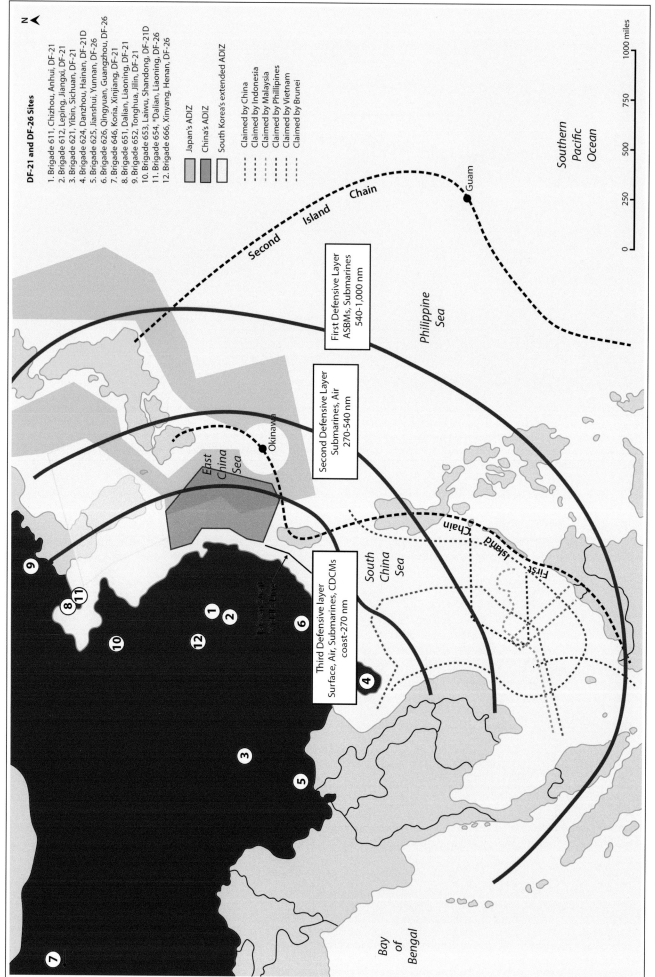

DF-21 and DF-26 Sites

1. Brigade 611, Chizhou, Anhui, DF-21
2. Brigade 612, Leping, Jiangxi, DF-21
3. Brigade 621, Yibin, Sichuan, DF-21
4. Brigade 624, Danzhou, Hainan, DF-21D
5. Brigade 625, Jianshui, Yunnan, DF-26
6. Brigade 626, Qingyuan, Guangzhou, DF-26
7. Brigade 646, Koria, Xinjiang, DF-21
8. Brigade 651, Dalian, Liaoning, DF-21
9. Brigade 652, Tonghua, Jilin, DF-21
10. Brigade 653, Laiwu, Shandong, DF-21D
11. Brigade 654, *Dalian, Liaoning, DF-26
12. Brigade 666, Xinyang, Henan, DF-26

Japan's ADIZ
China's ADIZ
South Korea's extended ADIZ

Claimed by China
Claimed by Indonesia
Claimed by Malaysia
Claimed by Phillipines
Claimed by Vietnam
Claimed by Brunei

N

Southern
Pacific
Ocean

0   250   500   750   1000 miles

Second   Island   Chain

Guam

First Defensive Layer
ASBMs, Submarines
540–1,000 nm

Philippine
Sea

Second Defensive Layer
Submarines, Air
270–540 nm

East
China
Sea

Okinawa

Chain

First   Island

South
China
Sea

Third Defensive layer
Surface, Air, Submarines, CDCMs
coast–270 nm

Bay
of
Bengal

(Map by Tom Cooper)

5
BLOCK, PARRY, SHIELD

The warhead of the DF-21D and its successors is meant to scream down from space and punch through the deck of a multibillion-dollar aircraft carrier. Western navies would like to end the missile's journey much sooner.

There are many options for stopping an anti-ship ballistic missile, and some of them may even work. The most obvious has already been tested and deployed against other types of ballistic missiles: early detection and interception. But more crucial for China's missileers, locating ASBM targets with enough accuracy to avoid needing to fire large volleys could prove an extreme challenge.

Staying Grounded

A so-called 'left of launch' approach is, of course, the best way to make sure no aircraft carriers encounter the business end of a ballistic missile strike. In this scenario, launchers for the DF-21D and its successors would be destroyed or disabled before the missiles took flight.

Cyberattacks can, in theory, remotely disable systems such as launch controls, or the communications equipment needed for the PLARF to send orders to its ASBM battery crews. Although the primary focus of US Cyber Command is, at least outwardly, to defend against attacks on American digital infrastructure, its foundational documents name-check China as a major adversary and say the command will 'prepare military cyber capabilities to be used in the event of crisis or conflict.'[1] In 2019, Defence Secretary Mark Esper confirmed that the command had developed offensive capabilities, without specifying what they might be.[2] Earlier that year, the US had for the first time acknowledged a cyberattack on a foreign adversary, using online weapons against Iran that 'disabled computer systems used by Iran's Islamic Revolutionary Guard Corps to control rocket and missile launches.'[3]

It is therefore probable that such capabilities also have been honed for use against a more advanced adversary like China. That country's systems are more advanced, robust and hardened against attack than Iran's, and the PLARF operates thousands of ballistic missiles, not just the DF-21D and DF-26, all of which have similar but not necessarily identical hardware and software to attack. Compared with conventional offensive actions, however, the blood and treasure costs of a cyberattack are small. That makes the odds high indeed that during a conflict, or in the run-up to one, US Cyber Command will make some attempt to disable China's missiles. The upside is high, the downside is low and when those two things are true, the odds of success are less important.

The more traditional means of stopping missiles before they are launched is to blow them up. The US military is one of a few on Earth, and the only one likely to get into a full-blown conflict with China, that can hit targets deep inside well-defended enemy territory. Its inventory of strike weapons is vast: Arleigh Burke and Ticonderoga-class warships can carry as many as 122 BGM-109 Tomahawk missiles; B-52s, B-2s and B-1s can carry the AGM-158, a low-observable air-launched cruise missile; stealth aircraft like the B-2, F-22 and F-35 can carry smaller precision weapons, including the GBU-39/B Small Diameter Bomb, which can glide to their targets from standoff ranges and whose small warheads are plenty big enough to mangle the important parts of a ballistic missile or its launch platform. If Conventional Prompt Global Strike, a US program to put non-nuclear payloads on intercontinental ballistic missiles, ever gets fully off the ground, it will be an option too. In theory, such a system could deliver a cloud of hypervelocity flechettes, cluster munitions or even just a fast-moving package of conventional explosives in the time it takes for the missile to get from its silo in the United States – a half-hour or less.[4] Flight tests of re-entry vehicles for such a system have been ongoing, and more than a billion dollars is budgeted for research and development in 2021.[5] But using such a weapon is problematic, especially against a nuclear-armed adversary such as China. It is difficult to imagine China's military or civilian leadership tracking intercontinental ballistic missiles headed for the homeland and not deciding to launch a retaliatory strike before the first detonation. A volley of conventionally armed ICBMs might thus lead to a nuclear exchange.[6]

That makes the safest means of directly attacking ASBM launchers standoff missiles or deep-penetrating airstrikes. But the safety is

The USS *Ronald Reagan* (CVN-76) carries aircraft for strike, electronic warfare, reconnaissance and air defense, among many other roles. (US Navy)

B-2 bombers and F-35 fighters would be among the high-end weapons used to 'kick in the door' and prevent China from launching its ballistic missiles, if planners chose that option. (US Air Force)

relative. Despite China's no-first-use stance, there remains some risk of a pre-emptive strike on the Chinese mainland triggering a nuclear response: 'China in some conditions may have incentive to launch a warning shot of a nuclear missile... to intimidate the enemy into halting an attack.'[7] And American firepower would have to travel deep inside China to hit DF-21D and DF-26 units. The launchers are mobile and can typically motor hundreds of miles without refuelling.[8] They are often based relatively near to the coast, in China's Hainan and Shandong provinces,[9] or in the country's northwest,[10] a vast desert region with hundreds of miles of integrated air defence networks between it and the border; DF-26 batteries have also reportedly been placed in the country's east.[11] Some strike routes can bypass the mainland's layered defences but require long flights over countries that probably do not want to get roped into a brawl between two superpowers.

China is also exploring how to mount ASBMs on its Type 055 Renhai warships,[12] giving them the theoretical ability to hold other countries' navies at risk at extreme range, albeit with even more targeting challenges than their land-based ballistic brethren. It is worth noting, however, that this sounds scarier and more advanced than it may actually be: the US Navy's RIM-174 SM-6 missiles can engage surface targets as well, and when their motors are expended, they, too, are anti-ship ballistic missiles.

Assuming the geopolitical obstacles can be overcome, the next question is one of math: if China fields more than 100 launchers for DF-21Ds and DF-26s, a US strike whose only purpose was to put ASBMs out of commission would require a significant chunk of America's cruise missile arsenal, its stealth assets or both. Even an attack on the roughly two dozen DF-21D launchers[13] would require a big stick. For flight crews, that means a high-risk mission, taking them through or near the defensive teeth of one of the most heavily armed countries on the planet. Using cruise missiles instead would put ships, subs or heavy bombers at risk, even at standoff distance, and would require them to get in strike range unnoticed and unmolested by the PLAAF's hundreds of air superiority fighters. Any such attack would require near-perfect targeting information. It is, in short, doable but difficult. And it is predicated on the idea that the risk and the potential losses of such a mission are worth it to hamstring just a single means by which China can hold carriers at risk; even without ASBMs, it has a navy of formidable

Transporter-erector launchers drive through the desert in China in preparation for an exercise. The DF-21D and DF-26 are both stored on and launched from such vehicles, making it more difficult to hit them in a pre-emptive strike. (eng.chinamil.com.cn/)

The Arleigh Burke-class guided-missile destroyer USS *Curtis Wilbur* (DDG-54) fires a 5-inch gun during a gunnery exercise. Burke-class ships also carry dozens of missiles for both land attack and air defense. (US Navy)

of a war. Aircraft are trackable via their emissions and radar returns, and it is unlikely a Chinese aerial platform, crewed or autonomous, could make it through a wall of Aegis-equipped warships and AWACS patrols to pinpoint a carrier's location. Ground-based over-the-horizon radars cannot generate an accurate enough location for a strike on their own (see Chapter 3). That is why China will most likely rely on satellites to provide targeting data.

The country has recorded scores of satellite launches since 2011, and since 2006 has put at least seven synthetic-aperture radars and at least 10 electro-optical sensors in orbit[18] – both of which types are suitable for hunting aircraft carriers. This observation network is primarily focused on China's neighbours and the South China Sea. Enough are in orbit that coverage is robust, if not continuous,[19] and warship-sized targets can be easily discerned if they are looking in the right place (See Chapter 4). Even without an arsenal of ASBMs, such satellites provide China with early warning and planning capabilities that could prove invaluable in a war. For the DF-21D, the satellites are essential: without them, the missiles most likely stay on the ground, or must be fired in such large numbers that most are wasted. That makes the satellites attractive targets for Western war planners.

Bringing war to space is not easy and carries an escalatory risk that other domains do not. Some aspects of space warfare are prohibited by international agreement; the Outer Space Treaty, of which the United States and China are both signatories, bans weapons of mass destruction in space, and the use of celestial bodies for military purposes.[20] Shooting down satellites, however, is not prohibited, and many countries have tested weapons that can do just that. It is a simple geometry problem: satellites tend to follow set paths at set altitudes, and an interceptor just has to arrive at a fixed point in space. The US first pulled off the feat in 1959, when a modified WS-199B Bold Orion air-launched ballistic missile passed within nuclear blast radius of a satellite in orbit. In 1985, an F-15 launched a purpose-built weapon, the ASM-135, and destroyed an aging NASA satellite.[21] In 2008, a RIM-161 Standard Missile 3 was used to destroy another American satellite in an operation called Burnt Frost.[22] The US Air Force also fields the X-37B, a robotic spaceplane whose capabilities and mission are opaque, but which has set several records for time spent in orbit before returning to Earth. One of its rumoured missions is tinkering with or disabling enemy satellites, although the scale of sabotage needed to blind China seems far beyond the capability of one uncrewed space vehicle.[23]

size,[14] including attack submarines and an unknown but immense number of conventional anti-ship missiles. Most likely, an attack on China's ASBMs would be part of a larger air attack on other assets and installations – an opening move or riposte at the start of what would seem fated to become an all-out war.[15] Further complicating matters, the DF-26 can be fitted with both conventional and nuclear payloads, meaning the fleet could be the unappreciative recipient of an atomic strike but not know for certain without finding out the hard way.

Lofty Ambitions

What if some of the ASBM launchers survive a pre-emptive US attack? Or what if China shoots first, launching all available ASBMs at US carriers in the South China Sea? The options for how to deal with these ballistic vampires shrink as soon as the missiles take flight.

In theory, ballistic missiles are vulnerable in the moments after they take flight but before they hit multiples of the speed of sound. If approached from the right angle and altitude, a conventional air-to-air missile such as an AIM-120 AMRAAM can destroy or cripple the critical flight systems that are working hard to get a DF-21D above the atmosphere and onto a ballistic trajectory.[16] Pumps, engines, guidance systems – all are under much more stress in the thick lower atmosphere, and the ballistic missile is flying in a straight line, relatively slowly, generating a huge radar return and infrared signature. But getting an aircraft in position to launch that air-to-air missile is as hard as scoring a hit is easy. The location of China's ballistic missile arsenal means a US aircraft would have to not only be flying deep inside mainland China, surrounded by air defence search radars, but *loitering* there, waiting for a missile launch. The odds of success are slim; the odds of survival are microscopic.

But far above China, and the South China Sea, the country's ASBM arsenal has another potential vulnerability. As noted in Chapter 3, precise targeting data is crucial to steering a DF-21D toward a carrier strike group. Chinese aircraft and submarines can potentially share such information with PLARF batteries, but it is a risky proposition: China's submarines are not as advanced (and therefore quiet) as their Russian and American counterparts.[17] An aircraft carrier's escorts would be on high alert for undersea threats in any sort of near-conflict atmosphere, and certainly in the midst

The most recent country to destroy a satellite is India, which in March 2019 used a Privthi Defense Vehicle Mk II to shatter a target it had launched earlier that year. The test was successful but illustrated how such an attack could create an unpredictable debris field.[24] That is a relatively small issue when it is just one satellite getting blasted out of near-Earth orbit. But if five, or 10, or dozens must be destroyed to sufficiently degrade China's missile targeting ability, the

The Arleigh Burke-class guided-missile destroyer USS *Curtis Wilbur* (DDG-54) has conducted freedom of navigation operations in the South China Sea, including transits of the Taiwan Strait. (US Navy)

debris problem becomes much larger and more dangerous. Planners might deem that an acceptable risk, but orbital debris is a widely studied concern.

The escalatory risk of an anti-satellite attack is another potential problem. The US National Reconnaissance Office has put 27 new satellites in orbit since 2011, and many pass over China in such a way that they would be vulnerable to China's own anti-space missile: the SC-19, a derivative of the DF-21. China tested the system in 2007, destroying one of its own defunct weather satellites.[25] The country is also suspected of testing an enhanced version of that missile, meant to reach objects in geostationary orbit, more than 22,000 miles above the Earth's surface. American attacks on Chinese satellites would almost certainly provoke retaliation in kind, although there is likely to be a first-mover advantage in that whoever disrupts the enemy's satellites first will make it more difficult for them to respond, even in space. The destruction or blinding of China's reconnaissance satellites would not only make it difficult for ASBMs to find a carrier strike group, but for China to respond effectively with any element of its military, at least right away. That makes such an opening move an attractive, if potentially dangerous, option.

Even if satellites and other intelligence, surveillance, target acquisition and reconnaissance, or ISTAR, assets are still functioning when DF-21Ds or other ASBMs are in the air, there is still a chance to disrupt the way they communicate with each other and with control nodes. Electronic warfare, at its simplest, is signal jamming, and such a capability could be used to confuse or degrade the capabilities of Chinese air or sea assets near an American fleet. On the surface, US Navy warships are equipped with the AN/SLQ-32 electronic warfare suite, which its manufacturer, Raytheon,

boasts has '100 percent probability of intercept' of any enemy radar emissions outside the range at which they can detect the ship.[26] This enables theoretical jamming of enemy airborne sensors, or vectoring aircraft to destroy them (launching a Standard Missile to destroy an airborne threat would entail activating the ship's fire-control radar, which would give away its position). In the air, all US carriers have a squadron of five EA-18 Growler electronic warfare aircraft aboard. These aircraft, developed from the F/A-18E/F Super Hornets, have a variety of integrated electronic warfare equipment aboard, a low radar cross-section, and the capability to carry other systems such as the ALQ-99 and Next Generation Jammer pods. Although the ALQ-99, especially, is a dated design and has reliability issues, Growlers could at the very least provide precise data for attacks on Chinese airborne ISTAR assets, if not jam them outright.

Cyberattacks could, as noted earlier, provide another level of electronic warfare if aimed directly at units controlling ASBMs. But a broader attack against communications infrastructure could deal a blow to China's ability to feed useful targeting data to its forces. US Cyber Command, other than its attack on Iran's systems, has been generally quiet about how far it can intrude into a state's infrastructure, including communications equipment. But other nations, such as Russia, have made public inroads in this area: Russian malware targeting US power systems, for instance, would have reportedly been able to switch off swaths of the grid.[27] It follows that such widespread outages would affect communications as well as creating a seemingly more urgent crisis to address than collecting ISTAR feeds from systems looking for American aircraft carriers.

The guided-missile cruiser USS *Port Royal* (CG-73), part of the USS *Makin Island* Amphibious Ready Group, steams through the South China Sea. (US Navy)

Flying Blind

Some sources suggest the DF-21D will get updated targeting information in flight.[28] If accurate, one of the most intriguing ways in which electronic warfare could cripple an ASBM attack is by attacking the warhead directly, either by thwarting the missile's ability to communicate or jamming its onboard radar. There is already a brief window, perhaps a minute long, in which a re-entry vehicle is shrouded in plasma created by the friction heat of its re-entry. The plasma blocks radio waves and can leave the warhead 'in the dark' until it slows down enough for the plasma to dissipate.[29] If the re-entry vehicle were to emerge from the plasma shroud and have no updated targeting information, it would be forced to rely only on its onboard sensors for its terminal phase of flight. The former Soviet Union's R-27K used passive guidance – homing in on emissions from a US fleet – to find its way to the target. But an ASBM using more active means, such as radar, to hunt for an aircraft carrier might be vulnerable to interference. Blasting its radar antennas with jamming energy could blind the system or reduce its effectiveness. The incoming ASBM warhead's location overhead would be no secret to the carrier strike group by that point, assuming US Navy systems were not themselves jammed. A direct attack on airborne communications systems and radar receivers is well within the capabilities of the fleet's ships and aircraft, although to date no such process has been publicly tested

against a ballistic missile warhead. The US Missile Defense Agency in early 2021 awarded contracts to L3Harris and Northrop Grumman to develop sensors capable of tracking hypersonic weapons from space, including manoeuvrable warheads.[30]

The DF-21D may have other tools for accomplishing its mission. An optical sensor – searching for recognizable patterns such as a wake or the carrier itself – could do the trick. Shielded from the initial heat and light of re-entry, it would open its eyes during the last part of the terminal phase, scanning thousands of kilometres of ocean as the re-entry vehicle streaks from 65 kilometres' altitude to sea level in less than a minute.[31] This sensor would most likely see in the infrared spectrum as well as the visible: if the physical bulk of a supercarrier is not enough to set it off from the ocean around

If anti-ship ballistic missiles rely on infrared or electro-optical sensors, a shipboard laser system like the Laser Weapon System could be used to blind or disable them. (US Navy)

it, its heat emissions against a backdrop of cool water will be. But even electronic eyes can be blinded. Although dazzling lasers are, by treaty, prohibited for use against personnel, they are effective and widely used against systems. The US Navy fields the purpose-built ODIN dazzler and has begun deploying modestly powerful destructive lasers such as the 30kw AN/SEQ-3 on several ships,[32] including the types of missile destroyers and cruisers that make up a carrier strike group. That system only has an effective range of about a mile – a distance an incoming ballistic missile warhead would cover in about a second. But the follow-on Laser Weapon System Demonstrator Mk 2 Mod 0 is, at 150kw, five times more powerful; although neither would do much to damage a warhead hardened to withstand the unearthly heat of re-entry, such systems on paper have enough juice to fry optical sensors at longer ranges. More advanced laser systems are being tested ashore. The farther into the sky they can reach, the less time an ASBM will have to peer at the sea below.

Any modern missile will have inertial and coordinate-based targeting as well. It can safely be assumed that the DF-21D, DF-26 and other such systems would be programmed to aim themselves at the last position their target was expected to be at the time of impact. But even adding 10 seconds of such 'unadjusted' flight to the terminal phase of an ASBM attack might save a ship. A Nimitz-class carrier barrelling along at 35 knots will travel almost 600 feet in that time, and a sharp turn at the right moment means a blinded missile could splash harmlessly nearby.

Motion in the Ocean

Some sources have suggested that the distance an aircraft carrier can travel during the flight time of an ASBM is enough to make it difficult for the re-entry vehicle to spot its target. Whatever sensors it is using, its field of view is thought to create a search area with a diameter of 50 to 80 kilometres.[33] In the time it takes an ASBM to reach a distant carrier, perhaps 25 minutes, an American supercarrier at full speed will have moved about 27 kilometres. If the DF-21D or DF-26 have been fed accurate enough targeting data, it would appear difficult (but not impossible) to escape the warhead's sensors. Indeed, Chinese military researchers reached the conclusion in developing the DF-21D that 'under optimal conditions, the range of manoeuvrability approaches 100 kilometres, which is more than enough to cover whatever evasive manoeuvres the carrier would undertake.'[34]

But that assumes perfect targeting, and conditions in war are never optimal. Little is known about what systems China would use to pick an aimpoint for its ASBMs. Over-the-horizon radar arrays, of which China operates at least one, can spot surface targets at extreme range, but do not provide precise information. The targeting location circular error probable (CEP) for an over-the-horizon array is between 20 and 178 kilometres, meaning there is a 50 percent chance of the target being in a circle with that radius.[35] As noted in Chapter 3, even satellite images, which can provide a more exact location for an aircraft carrier, may in practice produce a large targeting area because of the time it takes to transmit that information to decisionmakers.[36] Meanwhile, the area that the warhead's seeker can scan may be somewhat smaller than the targeting location CEP. That means that to ensure a high probability that the ASBM will attack the target, China must fire multiple missiles – even dozens, depending on how accurate the targeting data is and how wide the warhead seeker's field of view is (see Chapter 4). And this calculation does not consider attempts to intercept the DF-21D or DF-26 mid-flight; if mission planners assume the US can destroy inbound ballistic missiles, they will most likely order multiple shots

no matter what China's sensor capabilities are. All of this means that no matter what the scenario, if China means to sink a supercarrier, it will put several missiles in the air, making an unpleasant and busy day for fleet defence.[37]

Desperate Measures

If ASBM warheads survive until the final seconds of their flight toward an aircraft carrier, a confounding array of deception and countermeasures lie in wait – although their effectiveness against ballistic missiles is very much in doubt. For decades, the US Navy has equipped warships with basic countermeasures such as deck-mounted chaff dispensers, which launch a billowing cloud of metal strips into the air some distance away from the vessel. The strips each produce a radar return several times larger than their own dimensions. Together, they create the illusion of an enormous target, and combined with processes such as illuminating it with a signal from the target ship to produce the illusion of movement, can be

The Nulka decoy, which hovers some distance away from its launcher and pretends to be a warship – drawing enemy missiles away from their targets – has never been tested against an anti-ship ballistic missile. (US Navy)

an effective decoy for a radar-guided projectile. For a missile programmed with the exact radar return of a supercarrier, or using synthetic apertures to create a visual picture, such a tactic might be only marginally effective compared with how it would confuse a less-sophisticated weapon.[38] To work at all, the chaff would have to be timed with precision during a phase of the attack that would last only moments: fire too late, and the warhead will not react to the new radar return. Fire too early, and the cloud dissipates, allowing the warhead to reacquire the aircraft carrier. Chaff also, of course, is not effective against optical sensors, which should have no problem picking up a supercarrier, nearly a quarter-mile long and 250 feet wide.

The Phalanx close-in weapons system was designed to shoot down anti-ship missiles. But it is not likely to be able to effectively engage an anti-ship ballistic missile at extreme angles and speeds. (US Navy)

Carrier strike groups carry a growing array of other sophisticated decoys, ranging from drones to floating radar reflectors. The AN/SLQ-49, for instance, is an inflatable hexagonal reflector about the size of a small car. Launched from a ship, it floats in the water or can be towed some distance behind. The reflector's design creates a huge radar return – the size of a warship – although it does not produce a signature that matches a specific type of vessel. It also does not overcome the visual sensor issue. But another large radar target in the water near a carrier could confuse a fast-moving missile just long enough to make a difference.

Many US warships also now carry Mk53 Nulka decoys: canister-stored rockets that, when launched, hover and move at a ship's pace away from the vessel. Nulkas are festooned with transmitters that pump out jamming and false radar returns, trying to seduce incoming warheads into an attack far from their actual target. Although they have not been tested against ballistic missiles, they have been used in combat: In 2016, US warships deployed a Nulka when they were attacked by anti-ship missiles off the coast of Yemen.[39]

The most modern decoy in the US Navy's arsenal is the ADM-160C MALD-N, a semi-stealthy drone whose only purpose is to confuse and redirect enemy attacks. The naval version is ship-launched and can loiter for hours, providing a long-duration umbrella for a carrier strike group that might not know when an attack will come. The MALD-N is, in essence, a jammer with wings. Onboard processors allow it to react to targeting radars in real time, and beam back signals that mimic whatever the attacker is searching for. Although the drone was designed to complement strike fighters – swelling their apparent numbers or posing as a fleet of heavy bombers while stealthy assets make the real attack – the naval version is configured to provide effective radar spoofing at sea. Against a ballistic missile, these capabilities may be marginal; a warhead's radar would only be active for a minute or so, after the re-entry plasma dissipates, and is traveling much faster than the search radar on an aircraft or ship. And as with other countermeasures, the MALD-N was built with other missions in mind and has not been publicly tested against an ASBM-type system.

The last line of defence for an aircraft carrier is not a decoy or distraction, but a destructive hail of 20mm cannon rounds or a flight of short-range missiles. All US Navy warships carry at least one of two variants of close-in weapons system, Phalanx CIWS or SeaRAM, both of which are computer-controlled and radar-directed. The Phalanx, built around the Vulcan rotary cannon, with a fire rate of more than 100 rounds per second, can put a dizzying cloud of steel on targets up to five nautical miles away. SeaRAM uses the same radar, sensors and software but spits out RIM-116 rolling-airframe missiles in place of cannon rounds at about the same effective range. Again, in terms of engaging a target plunging at five or six times the speed of sound, five nautical miles equates to an engagement time of just a few seconds. But one high-explosive shell meeting a re-entry vehicle may, through sheer kinetic energy, destroy or deflect the incoming ASBM. Phalanx systems have not been tested against ballistic missiles of this calibre – to fly 1,500 kilometres, an intermediate-range weapon must hit velocities far beyond that of a tactical rocket or even artillery shell. But ground-based Phalanx systems, dubbed the Centurion C-RAM (Rockets, Artillery, Mortars) have successfully destroyed dozens of small ballistic targets like rockets in battlefields throughout the Middle East. It is noteworthy, however, that during Iran's ballistic missile attacks on two US-operated airbases in Iraq in 2019 that C-RAM systems may have been present but did not shoot down any of the re-entry vehicles.

None of these point-defence systems or countermeasures was designed to defeat an ASBM, and none has been tested against that sort of an attack. Their effectiveness may be limited or non-existent, but all options are on the table when the risk is a supercarrier on the bottom of the South China Sea.

Take Your Shot

The most-tested means of preventing a ballistic missile from hitting an aircraft carrier is perhaps the most obvious: to shoot it down. Since the mid-90s, the US military has experimented with destroying ballistic missiles as they cruise above the Earth's atmosphere: the

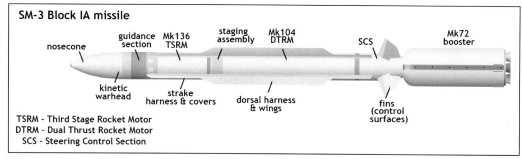

SM-3 Block IA missile

nosecone · guidance section · Mk136 TSRM · staging assembly · Mk104 DTRM · SCS · Mk72 booster

kinetic warhead · strake harness & covers · dorsal harness & wings · fins (control surfaces)

TSRM - Third Stage Rocket Motor
DTRM - Dual Thrust Rocket Motor
SCS - Steering Control Section

The SM-3 missile comprises a booster, an ascent stage with large guidance fins and the kinetic warhead, whose sensors guide the impactor in the final moments of an interception. (Diagram by Tom Cooper)

The Arleigh Burke-class guided-missile destroyer USS *John Finn* (DDG-113), part of the USS *Theodore Roosevelt* Carrier Strike Group, successfully intercepted an ICBM-class target in November 2020. (US Navy)

throw warheads off course or cause them to tumble and disintegrate on re-entry.

If the warheads made it into the thicker atmosphere, any of their decoys, such as balloons made to resemble re-entry vehicles or other radar reflectors, would fall away, leaving only real targets. That makes aiming at the warheads in their terminal phase much easier and was the thinking behind the other half of the Nike-X system, the Sprint missile. Within seconds of launch, it was moving at Mach 10, a velocity that could put it in space in half a minute. But it was never meant to get that high. At altitudes of at most 18 miles, the Sprint would detonate as close as possible to the incoming re-entry vehicle, its W66 warhead producing 'only' a few kilotons of yield, but an enhanced amount of radiation and X-rays, disabling the incoming nuke.

Even in the depths of the Cold War, planners saw fighting one type of nuclear fireball with another as too fraught of an approach. The entire system was only in service for one year in the mid-70s. US missile interception was more or less shelved for a decade, and when it re-emerged, it looked much different. Russia's modern anti-ballistic missile system, the A-135, has nearly 70 interceptors deployed around Moscow, all of which have nuclear warheads.[41]

The key problem with trying to shoot down a missile without using nuclear blasts is that the target is small – a cone the size of a large dog – and moving so fast that it can get from space to the ground in less time than it takes to sing 'The Star-Spangled Banner.' A re-entry vehicle that is manoeuvring because it is tracking a moving aircraft carrier, to pull an example out of thin air, further complicates interception.

So for the most part, modern missile interception doctrine focuses on the 'midcourse' phase of a ballistic missile's flight, in which it is no longer accelerating, but instead coasting above the atmosphere between launch and re-entry. Several factors make this an attractive proposition. First, because the incoming missile's velocity is constant, calculating where to aim an interceptor on course to hit it is easier. Second, there is no atmosphere, and the lack of drag means the interceptor can course-correct more precisely. Third, because the re-entry vehicle may still be attached to the upper stage of the missile or manoeuvring bus, the target is larger: hit any part of it, and the re-entry vehicle will tumble hopelessly off course even if it is not destroyed (unlike satellites, missiles broken up above the atmosphere should not spray dangerous fragments into orbit, as their trajectories will cause such debris to fall to Earth.) And of the three phases of a missile's flight, midcourse offers a much wider

so-called midcourse phase of a missile's flight. Fields of costly interceptors are stationed in Alaska and California, meant to deal with a small nuclear ICBM attack. But at sea, the US Navy has reconfigured many of its Standard Missiles to deal with ballistic missiles. They have been tested against an increasingly sophisticated array of targets and, as noted earlier, even used to destroy a satellite.

Planning around an interception is the reason the magazines of some carrier escorts are packed with SM-3 rounds, at the expense of offensive punch like Tomahawks. The exact weapons mix is classified, but some sources estimate only about 1/3 of a US Navy guided-missile destroyer's magazine is typically devoted to strike weapons.[40]

Killing a ballistic missile is not a trivial task. Early missile interceptor designs got around this difficulty by using nuclear warheads; even missing by a literal mile could be overcome if the blast radius were big enough. In fact, the first operational missile interception system, the Nike-X, used two different interceptors – one for high altitude and one for point defence – both with nuclear warheads. The high-altitude interceptor, the LIM-49 Spartan, could reach into space and carried what in modern times would be considered a city-busting thermonuclear payload: the five megaton W71 warhead. For the purposes of missile interception, it essentially meant a fireball more than 2 miles in diameter that would vaporize anything inside it and generate hard radiation and X-rays that would scramble any guidance systems that escaped. If the detonation occurred where there was enough atmosphere, a blast wave might

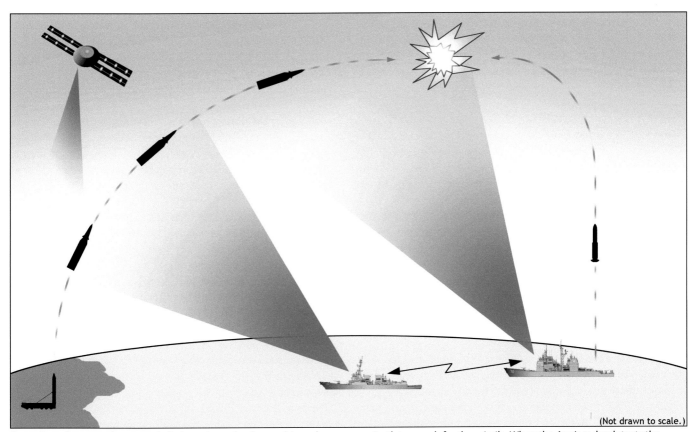

(Not drawn to scale.)

Space-based sensors detect a missile launch, cueing forward-based sensors on Earth to search for the missile. When the Aegis radar detects the missile on ascent, it provides targeting information to the 'shooter' ship, which can engage the enemy target in the midcourse phase much earlier than if it had used its own radar. (Diagram by Tom Cooper)

The USS *Lake Erie* (CG-70) launches an SM-3 interceptor at a ballistic missile target. The SM-3 can only attack targets outside the Earth's atmosphere, including anti-ship ballistic missiles. (US Navy)

'window' to hit the target than the boost and terminal phases – often as much as 80 percent or more of a missile's flight time.[42]

But an extra-atmospheric interception poses unique challenges as well. Because there is no drag, a radar-reflective balloon looks and behaves almost exactly like a real warhead. That means the interceptor and tracking stations must be able to discriminate between the two, or that many interceptors must be fired. And to reach the target's midcourse altitude of more than 100 miles, interceptors must be positioned in such a way that they maximize the area they can defend – creating a larger 'launch window' – and

radars must be positioned as close to the attacker as possible to make the window even bigger.[43]

The Aegis Combat System, designed to counter clouds of Soviet anti-ship missiles in the 1980s, was built around a powerful radar, the AN/SPY-1, set to be replaced starting in 2020 by the AN/SPY-6, which will be standard in Flight III Arleigh Burke-class destroyers. The detection range of the newest radar is a closely held secret, but aspects of it are purpose-built for spotting ballistic missiles.[44] The older-model AN/SPY-1 has been used in the interception of about 40 simulated targets in testing. However, none of the test targets so far have tried to manoeuvre or otherwise simulate what an ASBM strike would look like. As far back as 2011, the US Department of Defense noted that, 'A threat representative Anti-Ship Ballistic Missile (ASBM) target for operational open-air testing has become an immediate test resource need. China is fielding the DF-21D ASBM, which threatens US and allied surface warships in the Western Pacific.'[45]

The request has not appeared in the annual report of the office of the Director of Operational Test and Evaluation since then, and it is unclear whether a suitable target has been developed. But there has been no public test of a Standard Missile against a manoeuvring re-entry vehicle.

From a planning standpoint, however, that lack of testing might not matter. The bulk of America's missile interception infrastructure, hardware and software is built around the concept of shooting down ballistic targets in midcourse. As noted, warheads or their buses are coasting during that period, traveling on a path defined only by gravity and their own velocity. The capabilities of the re-entry vehicle in the atmosphere are therefore unimportant to the interceptor in space.

Bullets Killing Bullets

The carrier strike group's showpiece, the supercarrier, sails more or less in the centre of a ring of defence assets, including missile-armed warships of the Ticonderoga- and Burke-class, submarines and its own aircraft. At the edge of the circle closest to the potential ballistic missile threat would be at least one destroyer – not because of its missile loadout, but because of its sensors. That ship may also be in the best position to take a shot at inbound ballistic missiles,

but not necessarily; the shooter's interceptors cover a dome-shaped section of sky, and that dome creates a figurative 'shadow' of defence coverage on the surface. The better-placed the shooter is, the larger the coverage area is.

Placing ships closer to the enemy means their sensors can provide targeting data to the shooter ship much earlier than if it were using its own radar. That means interceptors can be launched earlier and allows for a 'shoot, look, shoot' engagement in which a commander can see whether the re-entry vehicle was destroyed and decide whether to fire again, rather than launching multiple interceptors at one target to ensure its destruction – a more efficient use of a ship's magazines.

Ideally, the fleet would get even earlier tracking data from other assets, such as satellites, which could detect a launch. Space-based radars could also provide early data on 'separation events,' in which missiles shed their early stages, payload shrouds and so on. Observing these events with high-frequency X-band radar, which provides resolution fine enough to spot details of the missile as well as a more precise trajectory, pours crucial data into the interception system. Modern ballistic missiles often employ decoys, separation debris and even deliberately created clutter such as explosively created, warhead-sized chunks of spent fuel tank to confuse radars. Observing each object come away from a missile can help software discern what is what.[46]

Even sophisticated decoys can be sniffed out. For instance: Mylar balloons in the exact shape and with the exact same radar return as a real re-entry vehicle do not have the same mass as a warhead. Because of Newton's second law, ejecting a warhead from the targeting bus will push the bus back with equal force. It requires

Successfully engaging an incoming ballistic missile means placing sensors far from the launcher, giving it more time and opportunity to engage. (US Navy)

The SM-3 has been successfully tested against an intercontinental ballistic missile-class target, as well as shorter-range missiles, but never against an anti-ship ballistic missile. (US Navy)

At that point, it is not using radar data at all: the kill vehicle is guided by an infrared sensor, which, when activated, should be staring in the direction of the target, and informed by in-flight data and pre-programmed information on the appearance of what it is trying to destroy. Traveling at several kilometres per second, it will steer itself toward the re-entry vehicle and attempt to hit it directly, demolishing the target with sheer kinetic energy.[48]

Last Chance

If the interceptor misses, engagement becomes easier in some ways – the confusing debris and decoys fall away in the atmosphere – but the margin for error shrinks to a razor's edge. And the SM-3, which is designed to kill targets outside the atmosphere, cannot engage the re-entry vehicle at that point.

The point-defence mission falls to the RIM-174 SM-6, which entered service in 2013 to replace the SM-2, although the older missile remains in some ships' magazines. It has a shorter range than the SM-3 because it does not need to reach space. Similarly, it does not kill with an impact; instead, it has a small blast-fragmentation warhead meant to shred a target with hypervelocity shrapnel when it explodes nearby. Unlike the SM-3, it is radar-guided all the way through – directed at first by ship-based sensors and then by its own seeker warhead.

SM-6 missiles have been successfully tested at least three times against ballistic missile targets.[49] But none of those targets was manoeuvring, as an ASBM warhead would while tracking a carrier. Unless future flight tests address that type of threat, it is unknown whether the SM-6 can knock an ASBM out of the sky in the same way it does an 'ordinary' ballistic missile. For now, the lack of a layered approach to defending aircraft carriers, and ships in general, from ballistic missile strikes seems like an important vulnerability.

New Hotness – Maybe

Emergent technologies will almost certainly add to a carrier strike group's ability to defend itself. Even the most high-power lasers will have little effect on the skin of a warhead built to survive the heat of re-entry, although they could blind its sensors. But railguns may offer an intriguing intersection of low cost, long range and deep magazines.[50] The weapons use high-powered electromagnets to accelerate a projectile to hypersonic speeds in the blink of an eye. A dense, 30kg round with no warhead traveling at Mach 7 at delivers kinetic energy equivalent to 2kg of TNT, but more important, would punch through a re-entry vehicle as though it were not there. A flechette-style round, designed to burst a second or two before reaching the target, would increase the chances of a shootdown; each dart can penetrate the armor of a main battle tank. Steerable rounds are an option as well, and the principal challenge is creating guidance systems that can withstand the immense forces (and electromagnetic fields) of launch. If that hurdle is cleared, a small, cheap round that can be guided to an incoming warhead by ground-based radar would provide terminal-phase defence at a fraction of the cost of an SM-6 shot. Because no propellant is needed to fire a railgun, a ship could theoretically carry hundreds, or even thousands, of rounds. This offers commanders the luxury of firing as many times as needed to hit an incoming missile.

This capability moved off the drawing board and onto the testing range. But after a series of high-profile, well-publicized test shots, the US Navy's railgun program went quiet. In mid-2021, the Navy removed funding for railguns from its budget proposal.[51] With future ships' powerplants being designed around the idea of

much less force to push away a balloon, and the resulting lack of bus reaction will also be recorded. Similarly, the balloons need to inflate, and if a piece of debris is observed to go from very small to warhead-sized, the system will assign it a higher probability of being a decoy. Even the sun's light affects the velocity and heading of an object in space – less of a factor in a shorter-range missile, but measurable when observing an ICBM.[47]

All this data streams back to the shooter ship, whether it is using its own sensors or relying on data from forward-based assets to 'launch on remote.' The system will then, if authorized, launch an interceptor at all the objects that are deemed a threat. For most of the interceptor's flight – and in most cases, this will be a RIM-161 SM-3 – a data link from the surface will guide it. Only in the last 30 seconds or so of the interception, after the kill vehicle separates from the final stage, is the interceptor on its own.

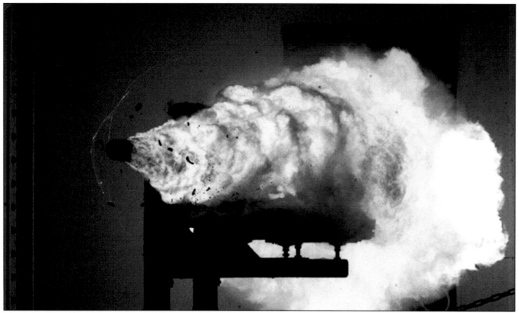

The US military has been testing railguns – which accelerate metal projectiles to enormous speeds using electromagnets – for more than a decade. (US Navy)

first place: 'the US Navy has a number of tricks up its sleeve.'[52] The most-tested method of stopping a ballistic missile remains attacking it directly, which obviates the advantages of a manoeuvring warhead and plays to the strengths of Western systems, which have been built and integrated, to a high degree, with thwarting a missile attack in mind. This can rapidly become a numbers game, with swarms of inbound tracks – from both ballistic and cruise missiles – demanding the attention of escort ships' full magazines. Future capabilities, from improved decoys and countermeasures to lasers and railguns, may tip the edge to the defender. But for now, a carrier strike group's best chance of avoiding an ASBM strike is to avoid detection or prevent accurate targeting. Some methods of doing that risk a quick escalation into space, and perhaps even nuclear weapons, because of the requirement to strike some of China's most-precious assets – and its home soil.

efficiency and excess power, however, such weapons will always be an intriguing option.

The challenges of defeating an ASBM are considerable, but so are the challenges of accurately aiming one in a search area encompassing millions of square kilometres. The United States, and other Western allies, have a wide array of ways to complicate an attack, starting with taking away the means of finding a carrier strike group in the

6

WHERE DO WE GO FROM HERE?

While US policymakers and naval strategists scramble to find solutions to the threat posed by the DF-21D, China is surging ahead with new missiles that push the PLARF's capabilities even further. Enter the Guam Killer. Like its smaller relative, the DF-26 IRBM made its first appearance on the streets of Beijing during the 3 September Victory Day Parade in 2015.[1] Sixteen missiles resting on their camouflaged TELs underlined the fact that Beijing's rocket forces are still a work in progress, increasingly capable but not yet satisfactory. And in case the messaging of Beijing's ballistic arsenal was not clear, the missiles' designations were painted on their sides in English characters, advertising new PLARF capabilities as they rolled down the promenades of the Chinese capital.

As with the DF-21D, the DF-26's anti-ship capabilities remain unknown. But its range of up to 4,000 kilometres puts the US territory of Guam within its reach, making it the only conventionally armed Chinese missile capable of reaching US soil. Home to critical American bases, including airstrips capable of supporting heavy bombers such as the B-52 Stratofortress, B-1B Lancer and B-2 Spirit, Guam is a critical outpost for America's Pacific strategy. After solving the issue of range, the DF-26's mission is much simpler if targeting an island almost 10 times larger than Washington, DC, rather than a manoeuvring warship.

Chinese statements in the last few years revealed that the missile is capable of carrying both conventional and nuclear warheads. This

fact, later corroborated by US Department of Defense assessments, does not make the DF-26 markedly different from several other ballistic missiles, but another of its features lays the foundation for a dangerous escalation dynamic. Other missiles in the DF series use their suffix to indicate the type of warhead each is designed to carry, and specific units are tasked with nuclear strike missions.[2] But the DF-26's warhead is hot-swappable, meaning it can be switched from conventional to nuclear on a launch-ready missile. That means that strategic planners must treat every DF-26 unit as if it were loaded with a nuclear payload. Its launchers are mobile, providing Beijing with a strategic strike force that can quickly disperse itself across China, complicating any plans the Pentagon might have for the destruction of China's land-based nuclear forces on the ground. And because every DF-26 launcher must be assumed to carry a nuclear warhead, American targeting must account for each – a number that may have already risen to more than 100. Targeting DF-26 launchers creates a use-it-or-lose-it scenario for Beijing: it will feel strategic pressure during a conflict to launch its nuclear missiles before they can be pre-emptively destroyed. The US could, for instance, conduct a limited strike against what American planners think are anti-ship missiles, but are actually nuclear-armed DF-26 TELs. Beijing could not afford to interpret that sort of attack as anything other than an attempt to neutralize China's nuclear forces and would respond with whatever of those weapons remained. The opacity surrounding

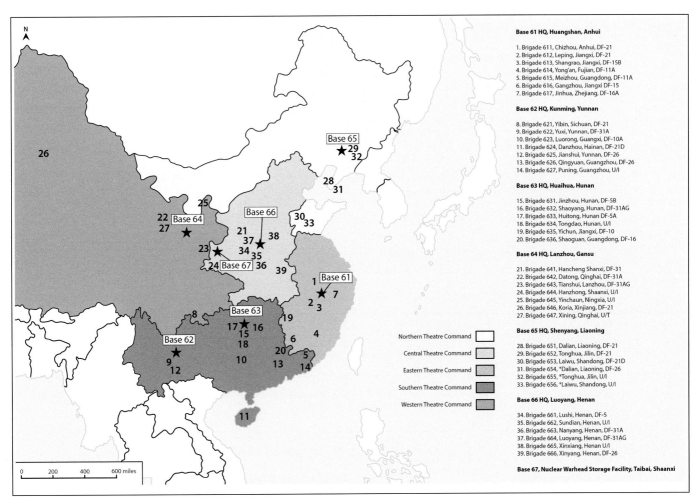

Base 61 HQ, Huangshan, Anhui

1. Brigade 611, Chizhou, Anhui, DF-21
2. Brigade 612, Leping, Jiangxi, DF-21
3. Brigade 613, Shangrao, Jiangxi, DF-15B
4. Brigade 614, Yong'an, Fujian, DF-11A
5. Brigade 615, Meizhou, Guangdong, DF-11A
6. Brigade 616, Gangzhou, Jiangxi DF-15
7. Brigade 617, Jinhua, Zhejiang, DF-16A

Base 62 HQ, Kunming, Yunnan

8. Brigade 621, Yibin, Sichuan, DF-21
9. Brigade 622, Yuxi, Yunnan, DF-31A
10. Brigde 623, Luorong, Guangxi, DF-10A
11. Brigade 624, Danzhou, Hainan, DF-21D
12. Brigade 625, Jianshui, Yunnan, DF-26
13. Brigade 626, Qingyuan, Guangzhou, DF-26
14. Brigade 627, Puning, Guangzhou, U/I

Base 63 HQ, Huaihua, Hunan

15. Brigade 631, Jinzhou, Hunan, DF-5B
16. Brigade 632, Shaoyang, Hunan, DF-31AG
17. Brigade 633, Huitong, Hunan DF-5A
18. Brigade 634, Tongdao, Hunan, U/I
19. Brigade 635, Yichun, Jiangxi, DF-10
20. Brigade 636, Shaoguan, Guangdong, DF-16

Base 64 HQ, Lanzhou, Gansu

21. Brigade 641, Hancheng Shanxi, DF-31
22. Brigade 642, Datong, Qinghai, DF-31A
23. Brigade 643, Tianshui, Lanzhou, DF-31AG
24. Brigade 644, Hanzhong, Shaanxi, U/I
25. Brigade 645, Yinchaun, Ningxia, U/I
26. Brigade 646, Koria, Xinjiang, DF-21
27. Brigade 647, Xining, Qinghai, U/T

Base 65 HQ, Shenyang, Liaoning

28. Brigade 651, Dalian, Liaoning, DF-21
29. Brigade 652, Tonghua, Jilin, DF-21
30. Brigade 653, Laiwu, Shandong, DF-21D
31. Brigade 654, *Dalian, Liaoning, DF-26
32. Brigade 655, *Tonghua, Jilin, U/I
33. Brigade 656, *Laiwu, Shandong, U/I

Base 66 HQ, Luoyang, Henan

34. Brigade 661, Lushi, Henan, DF-5
35. Brigade 662, Sundian, Henan, U/I
36. Brigade 663, Nanyang, Henan, DF-31A
37. Brigade 664, Luoyang, Henan, DF-31AG
38. Brigade 665, Xinxiang, Henan U/I
39. Brigade 666, Xinyang, Henan, DF-26

Base 67, Nuclear Warhead Storage Facility, Taibai, Shaanxi

Northern Theatre Command
Central Theatre Command
Eastern Theatre Command
Southern Theatre Command
Western Theatre Command

China's ASBM units are distributed around its vast territory. (Diagram by George Anderson)

Table 1: PLA Rocket Forces, Brigades by assigned Missile Type, 2020[3]

Type	Total	Type	No.	Brigade Designation & Missile Type
Nuclear	16	DF-4	1	662
		DF-5	3	631(B), 633 (A),661 (B)
		DF-21A	3	611, 612, 641
		DF-31	8	622 (A), 632 (AG), 641, 642 (AG), 642 (A/AG), 663 (A), 664 (AG)
		DF-41	1	644
		JL-2	-	four active Jin-class SSBNs with 12 launch tubes each
Conventional	9	DF-10*	2	623 (A), 635
		DF-11	2	614, 615 (A)
		DF-15	2	613 (B), 616 (A/B/C)
		DF-16	2	617 (A), 636 (A)
		DF-17	1	627
	10	DF-21	3	624 (D), 652 (C), 653 (D)
Dual	6	DF-26	6	621, 625, 626, 646, 654, 666
u/i	6	u/i	6	634, 645, 647, 655, 656, 665
Total number of operational Brigades: 40				
*Ground Launched Cruise Missile				

DF-26 warheads makes them a critical target but also a potential spark in a powder magazine of escalation.

A Numbers Game

The pace of the DF-26's construction also raises questions. The Defense Intelligence Ballistic Missile Analysis Committee in 2017 reported the number of both DF-21 and DF-26 launchers at approximately 16.[6] By the time the Department of Defense released its 2020 China Military Report, US estimates placed the number of IRBM launchers at 200. In fact, by the time of the 2020 report, it appeared by some interpretations that DF-26 production had exceeded that of the DF-21D. The exact wording gives an estimate

Table 2: PLA Ballistic Missiles by Type, 2020[4]

Type	Launch Preparation Time (min)	CEP (estimate in metres)	Number of Operational Brigades	Number of Units	Total Number of Launchers	Total of Number Missiles
DF-3*	120–150	1,000–4,000	10	-	-	-
DF-4	60–120	1,400–3,500	10	1	-	-
DF-5	30–60	500–800	6	3	18	18
DF-10	30	15	-	2	.	-
DF-11	30	200–600	10	2	20	80–120
DF-15	30	200–300	10	2	20	80–120
DF-15A	-	30–45	10	-	-	-
DF-16	10–15	-	-	-	-	-
DF-17		-	-	1	-	-
DF-21	10–15	100–300	10	6	60	200+
DF-26		-	-	-	-	-
DF-31	10–15+	5–10	8-10	7	56-70	32+
DF-41	-	-	-	1	-	16+
JL-1*	30	1,500–2,000	12	-	-	-
JL-2	30	300–500	12	4	4	48
*withdrawn from use	4–6 reloads are assumed for conventional ballistic missiles			- unknown or not available		

Table 3: Estimated Numbers of PLA Missiles and Operational Brigades, 2020[5]

	Type	Number/Unit	Number of Units (2020)	Total launchers	Total missiles	DOD Estimates	
						2019	2020
SRBM	DF-11	10	2	20	80–120	250/750–1,500	250/600+
	DF-15	10	2	20	80–120		
	DF-16	-	2	-	-		
MRBM	DF-21	10	6	60	240–360	150/150–450	150/150+
IRBM	DF-26	12	4+	48?		80/80–160	200/200+
ICBM	DF-5	6	3	18	18	90/90	100/100
	DF-31	8–10	7	56-70	56-70		

This table is based on two assumptions:

That the number of missiles (and thus launchers) per unit is correct, and

That there are 4–6 reloads for conventional, non-ICBM ballistic missiles. DF-26s have been shown reloading in December 2018, meaning that there should be at least one additional reload. ICBM-related estimates do not include JL-2s.

of Chinese IRBMs more generically within a paragraph mostly focused upon China's ASBMs.[7] If the reported ratio of IRBMs to launchers reflects the real strength of the PLARF's DF-26 capability, it implies the number of DF-21s has not budged. That vagueness in the Department of Defense's counting of IRBMs without specifically detailing the strength of the DF-26 force has contributed to a lack of consensus among the missile analyst community on what China's arsenal really looks like – other than being large, and growing.[8] The only conceivable reason for constructing so many TELs relative to airframes would be plans for continued growth toward a much larger missile inventory, and this is the assessment that appears more than once in the 2020 report.

This tracks with developments in China's naval shipbuilding program, in which vessels were procured and built in smaller batches while the designs were refined and adjusted. That created a

critical mass of available platforms without committing to a single early design. The DF-21D may have been the first step in China's anti-ship ballistic missile program, an opportunity to develop the supporting technologies required while using a missile airframe that was already in production. The rapid investment in DF-26 production and possible corresponding drop off in DF-21Ds rolling off the line may indicate the DF-21D was a steppingstone toward the intermediate-range missile, or that planners were satisfied with its performance and wanted to add a longer-range component in the DF-26, or that they did not see ASBMs as worth much additional investment. In any event, the DF-21D remains a potent pillar in China's defensive network – its range offers the PLARF overlapping ASBM coverage inside a 1,500-kilometre perimeter of China's coastline.

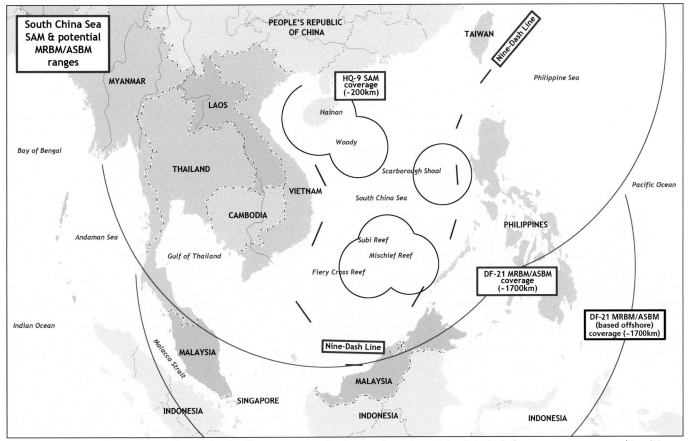

Installing ASBMs on China's man-made Spratly Island bases increases the distance from the mainland at which they can engage enemy ships. (Map by Tom Cooper)

Big Plans

But 1,500 kilometres from China's coastline might not be all that Beijing has in mind. From its considerable holdings in the South China Sea – heavily fortified bastions built up from undersea features – the PLARF could extend the reach of even the DF-21D considerably. Such a move would not come as a complete surprise.

One of its DF-21D units, the 624 Brigade, has been stationed at Danzhou on the PRC's Hainan Island, offering a commanding vantage point over the South China Sea. Beijing moved YJ-12B anti-ship cruise missiles and HQ-9B surface-to-air missiles to three of its reclaimed islands in 2018. With its reported range of 400 kilometres, the YJ-12B is itself a serious threat, and outranges the US Navy's own aging Harpoon missile. The addition of DF-21D to that mix would complicate American decision-making even further, creating interlocking fields of fire across millions of square kilometres of ocean. A move to Fiery Cross Reef, one of the three features that welcomed YJ-12Bs in 2018, would push the DF-21D's range to encompass critical

chokepoints and waterways with ease, creating a threat that must be reckoned with by any potential maritime rival as well as littoral states that might be asked to host said rivals.

As depicted above, if Beijing moves its ASBMs farther into the South China Sea, it would drastically change the security environment of the region. The Strait of Malacca and Singapore

The Arleigh Burke-class guided-missile destroyer USS *Benfold* (DDG-65), deployed with the 7th Fleet, sails through the South China Sea. (US Navy)

Strait fall within its estimated engagement range, enabling Beijing to threaten shipping and military movement through one of the world's major maritime chokepoints. Beijing's perpetual fear of encirclement places a premium on the ability to control those straits, as they are the primary conduit for the country's oil imports. A position on Fiery Cross Reef would also bring other strategic waterways like the Luzon Strait between Taiwan and Philippines, Indonesia's Makassar Strait, and the Sulu Sea into range. Although these bodies do not have the same geo-economic significance as the Strait of Malacca, in a war, these would be the claustrophobic corridors the US Navy would use to enter the arena. From its 'great wall of sand', the PLARF would pose a critical threat to any US effort to send ships inside the First Island Chain south of Taiwan.[9]

Stationing these missiles on small, isolated plots of sand might simplify the problem of targeting them, but enemy commanders would have to account for them regardless. The DF-26 amplifies the threat considerably, bringing over double the assessed range of the DF-21D. From Beijing's bases in the Spratly Islands, the DF-26 could target the east coast of India as well as northwest Australia, Korea, Okinawa, Japan, and of course, Guam. Again, forces stationed on China's South China Sea features are more exposed, but in order to target them effectively a US surface fleet would have to sail in range of punishing fire from DF-26 units on the Chinese mainland.

But Wait, There's More

Reports in 2020 indicated that the DF-26 was not just being trained on the seaward approaches to China, but potentially on distant seas as well. DF-26 units have been observed at Chinese bases in Xinjiang that put considerable portions of the Indian Ocean, as well as the Indian subcontinent, within their theoretical threat envelope. That positioning threatens all of rival India's major military ports and approaches despite China's having no Indian Ocean coastline of its own, creating new leverage for China and highlighting the multifaceted threat presented by the PLARF's missiles.

During a period of high tensions along the India-China Line of Actual Control (LAC) in January 2021, commercial satellite imagery revealed 16 DF-26 launchers deployed to a training site in China's eastern Shandong province, and to Xinjiang.[10] If a conflict erupts in which the PLARF takes aim at Indian ships in the Indian Ocean, Delhi would be faced with a significant challenge in deciding how to respond. Retaliation without attacking Chinese territory directly would be difficult, and an attack on China itself would be seen in Beijing as a considerable escalation. This scenario might be an outlier, but maintaining an anti-ship ballistic missile capability that covers the Indian Ocean is another step in China's efforts to implement its vision for 'far seas protection', and creates a paralyzing headache for Indian defence planners.

China's first overseas military base, opened in Djibouti in 2017,[11] is a reflection of Beijing's maritime priorities of securing the Indian Ocean and Arabian Sea for Chinese shipping and trade, but also anchoring the PLAN in the Indian Ocean Region to ensure strategic chokepoints remain open. The People's Liberation Army Navy has sent 36 counter-piracy task forces into the region since 2008, painstakingly building confidence and capability for projecting its power far from mainland shores. The Djibouti facility, it must be noted, is not a base in the sense that American forces would use. In fact, China officially takes particular care to refer to it as a facility rather than a base. There are no ships stationed there, nor visible naval combat capabilities. In comparison, the US Fifth Fleet resides on the island kingdom of Bahrain inside the Persian Gulf, with thousands of deployed sailors and significant numbers of warships

usually assigned, including US aircraft carriers and large-deck amphibious ships that often loiter in the Northern Arabian Sea and transit the Strait of Hormuz. There is no contest in maritime power in the region comprising the Horn of Africa and Persian Gulf region; the US Navy maintains superiority. However, Beijing's capability to launch the DF-26 into the region from western China complicates theatre dynamics in a way that has so far taken a back seat to considerations for its use in the eastern stretches of the Indo-Pacific. Already forced to reckon with Iranian ballistic missile capabilities on land and at sea – as evidenced by Iran's targeting of US forces in Iraq in 2020 – American planners must now also account for the threat posed by China's PLARF in the region. Although it may seem a remote possibility for now, it is worth considering the potential impacts of a PLARF DF-21D or DF-26 deployment to its base in Djibouti. As China's global interests grow, it is increasingly likely that its security footprint will too, and although China's overseas deployments have so far been limited, a look at the past 20 years of the PLA's development should be enough to convince any observer that the next 20 years might be equally surprising.

Another Arms Race

In war as in physics, every action has an equal and opposite reaction. As the PLARF continues to refine its anti-ship ballistic missiles, its potential adversaries race to develop countermeasures and their own offensive systems. This dynamic threatens to spill over into multiple domains, from the seas to space to cyber warfare. China's continued investment in intermediate-range ballistic missiles has shaken the foundations of arms control. In 2019, the United States withdrew from the Cold War-era Intermediate-Range Nuclear Forces treaty between the United States and Russia. Ostensibly, this was because Russia abrogated the treaty, but it also reflected the recognition that a major arms-control agreement that did not include China meant little, and offered China a significant security guarantee vis a vis Russia and the United States. After abandoning the treaty, the United States quickly began pursuing intermediate-range missiles that might be positioned along China's periphery. It is important to note that the 1987 INF treaty did not apply to missiles launched from ships or aircraft, so this particular dynamic is confined to land-based missiles.

At sea, the impacts of the DF-21D and DF-26 are of course even more pronounced. The very existence of anti-ship ballistic missiles has created a debate over the continued relevance of the aircraft carrier and its role as the focal point of American naval strategy. For now, the carrier's future still seems assured, but the way they are used will change. In the years between the end of the Cold War and this period of tension with China, the US Navy has operated without consideration for shore-based threats, given decades of focus on counterinsurgency wars in Southwest Asia. As a function of that freedom of action, the modern carrier air wing's operating radius has shrunk considerably. While a Cold War-era air wing was capable of flying sorties up to 1,800 nautical miles (nm) from the ship that launched them,[12] the modern carrier air wing's average range is under 1,300 nm when carrying their maximum payload and external stores.[13] The threat posed by the DF-21D and DF-26 is intended to keep American carriers at bay, which also negates the power of their embarked aircraft to strike at targets on land. That is one reason the US Navy is investing heavily in uncrewed carrier aviation: long-range drone aircraft that offer extended range and even in-flight refuelling for strike aircraft, and continued relevance for the modern supercarriers that the US Navy is only beginning to bring online in form of the Ford-class.

The United States wasted little time after leaving the INF treaty, testing a conventionally armed ballistic missile in December 2019. Such weapons would offer US forces another way to neutralize China's anti-ship ballistic missiles but increase the chances of unwanted escalation. (US Department of Defense)

The Digital Battlefield

Cyber weapons are another important facet to consider. The kill chain of ASBMs – the steps between finding a target and successfully attacking it – will be a primary target for anyone seeking to avoid being on the receiving end of an anti-ship ballistic missile. One way to break the chain is an extensive offensive cyber operations campaign before a single shot is fired, mapping networks, and creating plans for disruption. For the DF-21D and DF-26, the kill chain leans hard on communications and information technology, as signals pass between sensors and the launchers, and the missiles

and their ground stations. Offensive cyber operations offer a way to potentially disrupt those communications without the limitations of range or considerations for nuclear escalation posed by more conventional methods of disabling a missile. This could take several forms or follow multiple vectors of attack. First, it stands to reason that cyber operations might offer insights into the two missiles themselves, scooping up details on their vulnerabilities and shortcomings. Much as China has spent considerable time over the past decade pilfering secrets and technical data, so too might the United States.[14]

The guided-missile cruiser USS *Bunker Hill* (CG-52) is one of several US surface ships that have conducted freedom of navigation operations in the South China Sea. (US Navy)

If war breaks out, cyber operations might first try to gouge the eyes out of the sensors responsible for providing targeting data to the mobile launchers, preventing ASBMs from being aimed. Sensors on land and at sea – and especially in orbit – create significant potential for escalation across multiple domains, as no nation would be thrilled to discover its military's most sensitive systems were suddenly offline, trying repeatedly to divide by zero. Strategic cyber operations are thus extremely disruptive despite a lack of human casualties.

China's missile progress has also reinvigorated US efforts in ballistic missile defence. Although the US Navy has sailed with ballistic missile defence capability in the form of its Aegis combat management system for many years, ground-based missile defence is an increasingly popular option for defending against the DF-26. Accordingly, the missile carrying the 'Guam Killer' moniker has spurred US efforts at constructing an integrated missile defence system for Guam, intended to provide a security umbrella for the island territory. The efforts include Aegis Ashore, a land-based version of the Navy's successful ship-mounted air defence system, which has shot down ICBM-class targets in testing.

Good Business?

The question of proliferation also dogs China's anti-ship ballistic missiles. Selling the DF-21D or DF-26 to other nations seems unlikely for a number of reasons. The unproven capabilities of the missiles might be a challenge to marketing efforts, first. While the opacity surrounding them serves China's interests, it may not suit a customer's strategic needs. And should those capabilities prove less than advertised, China would lose the missiles' considerable deterrent value. Allowing proliferation via an export variant would also create vulnerability through exploitation, as no prospective customer could guard the missile's capabilities as effectively as China has to date. The United States has proven itself very motivated to hunt down adversary technologies for this very purpose, including scooping up an advanced Russian air defence vehicle from Libya in 2020.[15] However, there is precedent for the idea that some elements of China's anti-ship missile programs might make their way into the illicit defence market. Chinese sales of missiles and technology in the 1980s and 1990s gave birth to a robust Iranian missile program – one whose progress was illustrated in the January 2020 precision attack on Ayn al-Asad air base in Iraq. Though this cooperation ostensibly ended in 1998 with a promise from then-President Jiang Zemin to cease sales of anti-shipping cruise missiles or supporting technologies, Beijing's calculus may change in the event of continued worsening relations with the United States. Iran has claimed an operational anti-ship ballistic missile capability since 2011, and in 2021 the Islamic Revolutionary Guards Corps (IRGC) claimed to have used a new variant to target a platform at sea during its exercise Noble Prophet 15. In contrast to Chinese media, the IRGC released footage of a purported impact at sea, but the full capabilities of its anti-ship ballistic missiles (including whether it can hit a moving target) are unknown. China-Iran cooperation on refining technologies and tactics might be an outlying scenario, but it warrants consideration. A proven anti-ship ballistic missile with sufficient range would give Iran incredible leverage over the Strait of Hormuz, through which about 20 percent of the world's oil supply flows each year. A missile with capabilities commensurate with the DF-21D could range the entirety of the Persian Gulf and hold the US Fifth Fleet, along with its base in Bahrain, at risk.

Pick a Missile

With two anti-ship ballistic missiles now in service, it remains unclear whether China will press forward on production of both. Only two PLARF brigades were equipped with the DF-21D, and both of those units reportedly received an unidentified new missile in 2020, leaving some doubt as to the DF-21D's continued role as a front-line deterrent.[16] If it proves that these units, the 624 and 653 brigades, have transitioned to the DF-26, then it would confirm that the DF-21D was a stepping stone toward a more mature capability. That gains additional credibility when considering that specific units were created for operating the DF-21D, while there is no indication yet that DF-26 brigades are assigned to any specific subvariant of the missile or mission. Moreover, after more than a decade of service, the DF-21D rates only two dedicated units (which may have already been redesignated). The DF-26, on the other hand, boasts five (possibly six, according to some analysts) brigades, with far more to come if the estimate of 200 launchers is correct. Some analysts estimate each DF-21D brigade employs approximately 12 launchers, though authoritative numbers have not been made publicly available. If that number is accurate, 200 launchers would provide for up to 16 DF-26 units at the most aggressive estimates or eight at the lower end, an increase of two over the units known in 2021.

Although the DF-26 offers an increase in range, its ability to attack targets appears no different than that of the DF-21D. But future developments in China's anti-ship ballistic missiles might also include upgrades to the warhead. As has been noted already in this book, the problem of striking a moving aircraft carrier with a ballistic unitary warhead is no mean feat. A submunition warhead might be one way for the PLARF to increase the likelihood of a successful strike. Why would a hunter use a rifle to hit a flying target when a shotgun offers a wider spread, more likely to score a hit? Even a successful hit from a unitary warhead poses almost no chance of sinking an aircraft carrier unless it ignited catastrophic fires or secondary explosions. The 2005 SINKEX of ex-USS *America*, intended to produce insights into how the carrier's design would absorb damage – information that would be used to improve the US Navy's Nimitz-class aircraft carriers – illustrates some of the rationale for non-unitary warheads on an ASBM. That the decommissioned carrier remained afloat for four weeks before being scuttled has surely not escaped Beijing's notice.[17] Taking a carrier out of the fight without sinking it might even work in Beijing's favour, as American politicians would have a much easier time de-escalating from an exchange that did not cost American lives. Sinking a carrier, however, would almost certainly result in massive retaliation, followed by a declaration of war. As discussed in earlier chapters, the DF-21D and DF-26 are unlikely to hit a carrier, let alone sink it, without accurate massed volleys, and are more likely viewed as mission-kill weapons – capable of peeling open a flight deck, wrecking an aircraft elevator, or striking the bridge and its radar arrays. A submunition warhead increases likelihood of landing such a blow on a critical system, albeit a lighter one than would be achieved with a unitary warhead.

Defensive Moves

It is undeniable that anti-ship ballistic missiles pose a threat to naval vessels, but the targets are getting harder. Those countries capable of maritime ballistic missile defence will continue to invest in that capability, and both sides will continue to search for a decisive advantage. Indeed, the PLARF has not stopped at the DF-26. In 2019, PLA officials claimed to have begun work on an anti-ship variant of their hypersonic glide vehicle, the DF-17.[18] Hypersonic weapons travel slower than those relying on ballistic re-entry, but their high

A formation of Dong Feng-17 conventional missiles takes part in a military parade during the celebrations marking the 70th anniversary of the founding of the People's Republic of China (PRC) at Tiananmen Square in Beijing in 2019. (eng.chinamil.com.cn)

manoeuvrability and lower altitude flight make traditional methods of interception harder and reduce how long commanders have to make a decision compared with the flight times of typical anti-ship cruise missiles. Although the DF-21D and DF-26 are capable of manoeuvring in their terminal phase, the DF-17 is designed to undertake 'extreme manoeuvres' and 'evasive actions' according to US defence officials.[19] DF-17 tests were reported as early as 2014 and the missile made its debut at 1 October 2019 parade celebrating the PRC's 70th anniversary of its founding.[20] In that same parade, the world got its first glimpse of China's newest addition to its ballistic missile menagerie, the DF-100. Also referred to in some publications as the CJ-100, this missile's capabilities are largely a mystery, other than its purported ramjet propulsion.[21] Chinese media has referred to the missile as Changjian-100, or Long Sword, claiming that the missile 'can quickly break through the enemy's air defence network, accurately strike the enemy's large surface ships, and communication command hubs and other high-value targets.'[22]

The DF-17 and CJ-100 would not be engaged by the Navy's ballistic missile defences, but by missiles meant to kill targets in the atmosphere – most notably the SM-6, the most advanced air defence missile in the US arsenal. However, adding multiple missiles with varying trajectories, seekers, and terminal phases complicates an already-difficult task by saturating sensors and exhausting missile interceptor magazines. For the attacker, getting one past the goalie is enough to win the match.

Risk, Risk and More Risk

But why continue to create new anti-ship ballistic missiles? Conjuring up the ability to attack from multiple trajectories might be worthwhile in terms of overwhelming missile defence systems but seems to solve a problem readily be addressed by larger volleys of DF-21Ds and DF-26s. Despite the continued public emphasis on the PLARF's ability to strike at the American navy, some posit that striking ships with ballistic missiles is no longer a primary focus of China's strategy. Instead, they warn of a potential surprise attack on US bases, using precision warheads to destroy ships while they are at the pier and pounding critical shore support networks

into rubble.[23] There is some logic to this argument. China today fields a world-class navy that has already surpassed the United States in raw numbers. Although it lacks much expeditionary capability, it is no longer a brown-water force too weak to threaten American carriers. China's ballistic missile force not only has the capability to strike at every American base west of Hawaii, it appears to be training with such a strike in mind.[24] Even as early as 2013, the same collection of satellite imagery showing possible DF-21D tests against ship-shaped outlines in the desert also revealed targets simulating US bases, airfields, and vessels at China's ballistic missile impact ranges in western China.[25] In a 2017 computer-aided simulation, researchers at the Center for New American Security found that a pre-emptive Chinese strike on US bases in the Indo-Pacific could yield catastrophic results for the United States:

- Almost every major fixed headquarters and logistical facility struck, with key headquarters struck within the first few minutes of the conflict
- Almost every US ship in port in Japan struck pierside by ballistic missiles
- In most cases, cratering by ballistic missiles of every runway and runway-length taxiway at all major US air bases in Japan
- As a result of runway cratering, headquarters destruction, and air defence degradation, more than 200 trapped US aircraft destroyed on the ground in the first hours of the conflict[26]

By stripping away the safe havens the US would rely upon to fight a war, a surprise attack by the PLARF would cripple US warfighting capability in a manner akin to the aftermath of Pearl Harbor, but with even more dire effects. In 1941, US shipyards were robust and able to return many of the crippled ships to service. In 2021, US shipyards are few and limited in their capacity; as an example, it took two years to complete repairs to the USS *John S. McCain*, damaged in a 2017 collision.[27] New ships cannot be built with sufficient speed to replace losses as they were in the 1940s.

Predicting the future is hard, especially when dealing with a state that maintains such tight control over publicly available information regarding its military capabilities. But it is clear that Beijing's defence strategy will continue to feature ever-increasing numbers of sophisticated missiles. Whether these missiles are used to take aim at ships at sea or bases on shore, or a combination of both, their ability to menace US forces across the region cannot be discounted and will drive the defence planning of Beijing's adversaries until there is a thaw – or a war.

The USS *John S. McCain* is towed away from a pier in Singapore after initial repairs to damage it suffered in a collision with a commercial ship in September 2017. (US Navy)

CONCLUSION

The advent of the aircraft carrier may have made anti-ship ballistic missiles inevitable.

As US carriers, in particular, came to dominate the seas – starting in the Second World War and extending all the way to the present day, with carrier-based aircraft striking the Middle East – adversaries looked for ways to shred them. The Soviet Union invested in powerful submarines during the Cold War and built bombers and cruise missiles in huge numbers to overwhelm ships' defences. China's approach, spurred by the arrival in the 1990s of American carriers at its doorstep, just took the solution a step farther and carried the fight a greater distance from its shores.

US carriers provide striking power and maritime surveillance to the US and its allies that no other single weapon can match. Its fleets are built around them and it has poured billions of dollars into systems that can defend them – an effort that in recent years has extended into space. Any adversary looking to control the seas in its own backyard must first find a way to deal with American supercarriers. And traditional weapons, where the US has an advantage built and honed during its decades of Cold War with the USSR, do not offer much of a solution.

So China's ASBMs, for reasons political and strategic, are not going anywhere. They solve a problem and address what was at one point a serious dagger piercing the country's national pride. An asymmetrical response writ large, this 'assassin's mace' has altered the trajectory of strategic thinking in and around the Asia-Pacific region.

They are not the infallible weapons, however, that Chinese Communist Party leaders and media organizations might have us believe. As with any weapon developed to challenge a competitor, countermeasures and new operational behaviours have evolved to

greet this new threat. Cyberweapons to confound and delay the systems that communicate on land and in space, long-range strike options to attack missiles and their launchers on the ground, missile interceptors to swat incoming missiles down from their ballistic trajectories, and shipboard systems to throw up sheets of lead and missiles in a last-ditch defence – all have been incorporated into a layered bastion of security for the fleet's crown jewel.

No weapon is without vulnerabilities. China's anti-ship ballistic missiles are no exception. Their long kill chain, spanning the thick brambles of CCP bureaucracy, difficult targeting processes, the cold vacuum of space, and their final plasma-coated trajectory all offer vectors for an opponent to disrupt an attack. And the DF-21D and its cousin the DF-26 are not completely revolutionary systems; rather, they are largely composed of improved versions of technology that has existed in some form or another for decades.

Media-fuelled hype might offer the impression that killing an aircraft carrier is a one-missile job. That could not be further from the truth. Even if the missile's touted capabilities work as advertised, a successful attack will most likely exhaust a not-insignificant portion of the Chinese ASBM magazine. And even an unsuccessful attack will invite significant retaliation. But a carrier taken out of action is a serious risk – one that China's adversaries must take seriously even as Beijing carefully cultivates an air of dangerous mystery surrounding the missiles.

What can the West do about them? Until there are missiles in the air, that is likely to be an open question. The most optimistic but least probable scenario is that DF-21Ds and DF-26s turn into expensive telephone poles when the launch key is turned, neutered by cyberattacks. The United States has invested heavily in such capabilities and deployed them from time to time against its main adversaries, including Russia, Iran and even China (one such operation extracted the personal details of Chinese operatives in PLA Unit 61938, a hacking detachment, and publicly charged them with stealing secrets from US companies). The stakes are too high to rely on volleys of code to knock down enemy missiles, however, so the next step up the ladder is to make sure those missiles are flying blind.

Destroying or disabling satellites or radars is an escalatory move in its own right. Wrecking anything in orbit creates debris that can lead to problems with friendly satellites, retaliatory attacks and even big-budget sci-fi movies with questionable physics. But there is no question that satellites play a crucial role in China's ability to aim its ASBMs. Without them, it is stuck with ground-based sensors – for the most part, the only radars that can peer deep enough across the ocean to spot warships before they are in range of more conventional weapons do not have enough precision to aim the missiles on their own. Putting planes in the air around a hostile US carrier is, in a modern combat environment, mostly just an invitation for a face-to-face meeting with a Standard Missile.

So 'kicking down the door' in advance of a carrier strike group's passing through it is one way to handle the situation. A supercarrier and its escorts might not be able to get close enough to apply their own foot, but other weapons, from cruise missiles to malicious code, may get the job done.

The US is also trying to catch up to China on its own ballistic playing field after scrapping the Intermediate Nuclear Forces treaty. The pact between the US and Russia was ostensibly to eliminate one leg of the nuclear arms race. But a side effect was that it prevented both sides from developing ballistic missiles with less than intercontinental range. With those constraints removed – and with a desire to get China's missiles off the board before they are off the ground – American weaponeers are pouring resources into creating conventional ballistic missiles that can be deployed around Asia, offering the means for a crippling first strike or a counterpunch in the aftermath of a Chinese strike that demolishes many of the other assets the US had planned to use in a regional war.

One minor problem with that approach is the similarities it has to a nuclear exchange. In the history of war, there has never been a large-scale exchange of nuclear missiles. Indeed, during the Cold War, the only discussion of such a scenario involved city-busting nukes, and the central question was whether it made more sense to launch on warning (without confirming a nuclear strike was under way) or to wait until some mushroom clouds appeared before launching an all-out retaliation. In a sense, it was academic; both scenarios involved what amounted to the extinction of at least two large nations. In the modern Asia-Pacific theatre, it is not academic in the slightest. A hail of ballistic missiles – especially when China's DF-26 can be conventional or nuclear, with no way of telling until impact – requires a decision in the short time they are in the air. Officially, the US policy is to respond to a nuclear attack after the fact; eliminating the country's nuclear arsenal, spread among subs, bombers and silos, is an impossibility. Unofficially, no one knows how the opening moments of a regional war would look.

Worse, an American pre-emptive strike on China's ASBM arsenal would require hitting DF-26s – some of which are nuclear-armed. Would China tolerate an attack on its strategic forces? Or would commanders think they were faced with a use-it-or-lose it scenario and put their nukes in the air to avoid the possibility of the country's most potent weapon being put out of commission in the face of a superior force? Absent perfect intelligence about which launchers carry which type of warhead (warheads that can be swapped in

the field), there is no way to pre-emptively take China's ASBMs off the board – especially using American ballistic missiles – without raising the risk of a nuclear conflagration. In that way, destroying the sensors and communications used to aim the missiles might be the least-risky way to make sure US supercarriers can sail through the South China Sea as they wish, if not the most effective.

But carriers are not the only targets, and door kicking is not the only answer. The same precision capabilities that enable a theoretical bullseye on a moving ship can also hit a large, stationary target with relative ease. US bases around the region are well within range of the DF-26, and the missile's growing numbers means an expanding threat to those facilities – far beyond the ability of US air defences to handle. One solution to that problem is dispersal. Just as in infantry tactics, a group of targets is an opportunity; targets spread apart divide attention and resources. Adding friendly ports, airfields and repair facilities gives the United States a little breathing room, in theory, at least in the sense that some firepower would survive a Chinese first strike. And of course, a lot of US firepower exists outside of China's missile range in any event. With 11 supercarriers, there are always more air wings to bring to the theatre. But pouring more warships and fighters into the Asia-Pacific (or Indo-Pacific, in the parlance of the US military) region still leaves the problem of where they go to refuel and rearm. Complicating matters is that one of the most likely flashpoints for a conflict, a Chinese invasion of Taiwan, is time sensitive. China would be unable to take and hold a useful part of Taiwan in hours, or even a day or two. But beyond that, the horizon becomes much darker for Taipei. China, just dozens of miles away, can keep throwing ships, troops and missiles at Taiwan until the defences and defenders are exhausted. A swift American arrival on the scene is not just a hope, but a requirement for Taiwan to survive such an attempt. Dispersing US forces around the region or holding them just outside China's missile range might inadvertently achieve the strategic goal of delaying reinforcements.

Regardless of where its ships are, the United States will continue pouring money into missile and air defence systems. Aegis has now been tested against missile targets all the way up to the faster, more complex ICBM level. The shore-based system is well on its way to deployment around Asia, including Guam and Japan. On the offensive side of the coin, China will continue developing new missiles and perhaps even modifying the ones it already has. Cluster munitions might widen the kill envelope of its ASBMs, making it easier to hit a critical aircraft carrier system, if not sink the ship. And new missiles, including the arrowhead-shaped DF-17 and ramjet-powered CJ-100 – not to mention ship- and air-launched versions of the DF-21D, if those become operational – offer new and exciting (if untested) ways to deliver lethal force to the hulls of American vessels.

At any rate, even if the DF-26 is no different from the DF-21D in any way other than range, it changes the strategic picture. This is true for other potential Chinese adversaries such as India, whose ports and eponymous ocean are all in range. The Persian Gulf, too, falls under the deadly umbrella of the DF-26, which is unfortunate for the US Navy and a large chunk of the world's oil shipments, both of which want to continue operating without missile-sized holes in their decks.

Elsewhere in the Persian Gulf, Iran may be interested in talking business with China about buying DF-21Ds. Iran's own precision ballistic missiles have already caused literal headaches for US forces in the region and adding a more advanced capability would be a major step. Regardless of how much money is on the table, it is unlikely such a deal would go forward, however. For China, the chances of one of its missiles falling into US hands, or failing in combat, are too high.

But above all else, China seems committed to expanding its arsenal. The number of DF-26s and launchers is heading to the hundreds, or at least a greater number than can be easily targeted by Western strike planners. It is not publicly known how many of those missiles will carry ASBM warheads. That makes it impossible to say whether China is expanding that aspect of its arsenal, and, by extension, how important anti-ship ballistic missiles are to Beijing's war plans or whether the military is confident in their effectiveness.

But as noted above, no matter what, the ASBM component is a niche aspect of the arsenal relative to the ability to hit fixed targets around the region.

China's 'carrier killers' may never take flight in anger, and might not be effective if they do. But their precision capabilities and growing numbers mean far more than America's flattops are being held at risk. Although the potency of US supercarriers is undimmed, barring technological advances, their ability to sail carefree around Asia in a conflict and find a safe harbour – let alone motor through the Taiwan Strait – is already dead.

BIBLIOGRAPHY

Primary Sources

Bai, Bowen; Liu, Yanming; Lin, Xiaofang; and Li, Xiaoping, 'Effects of a reentry plasma sheath on the beam pointing properties of an array antenna', *AIP Advances* 8 (2018), p.1

Confidential subject matter expert, interview by author, Singapore, 8 December 2020

Confidential technical source, interview by author, Singapore, 1 September 2020

Halifax International Security Forum, *#HFX2020: Admiral Philip Davidson* [video] (Halifax International Security Forum, uploaded 20 November 2020) https://youtu.be/7q5mvRJyGrw?t=1238, accessed 17 January 2021

Headquarters of the Department of the Army, *The Pershing II Firing Battery* (Washington, D.C., 1985)

LaFoy, Scott, personal correspondence, 4 September 2020

Lewis, Jeffrey, Director, East Asia Nonproliferation Project, interview by author, Singapore, 5 January 2021

Li, Le-Wei, 'High-Frequency over-the-horizon radar and ionospheric backscatter studies in China', *Radio Science*, 33:5 (1998), pp.1445–1458

Luo, Junhai; Han, Ying; and Fan, Liying, 'Underwater Acoustic Target Tracking: A Review', *Sensors* (2 January 2018), pp.8–9

Makeyev Rocket Design Bureau, 'Rocket R-27K', Makeyev Rocket Design Bureau, <http://www.makeyev.ru/activities/missile-systems/2/RaketaR27K/>, accessed 15 February 2021

Mastro, Oriana Skylar, Center Fellow at the Freeman Spogli Institute for International Studies, Stanford University, interview by author, Singapore, 3 February 2021

Outer Space Treaty (New York, NY, United Nations, 1966)

Raytheon, 'AN/SLQ-32(V) Shipboard EW System', *Raytheonmissilesanddefense.com* (2020), <https://www.raytheon.com/capabilities/products/slq32>, accessed 24 April 2020

Raytheon, 'U.S. Navy's SPY-6 Family of Radars', *Raytheonmissilesanddefense.com* (2020), <https://www.raytheonmissilesanddefense.com/capabilities/products/spy6-radars>, accessed December 2020

Raytheon, 'SM-6 Missile', *Raytheonmissilesanddefense.com* (last modified 4 April 2020), <https://www.raytheonmissilesanddefense.com/capabilities/products/sm6-missile>, accessed 6 June 2020

Stefanovich, Dmitry, research fellow, Center for International Security, Institute of World Economy and International Relations of the Russian Academy of Sciences, interview by author, Singapore, 4 February 2021

Stokes, Mark, executive director, Project 2049 Institute, personal correspondence, 12 February 2021

Xie Yu, Pan Liang and Yuan Tianbao, *Trajectory Planning for Reentry Maneuverability* (Changsha, China, National University of Defense Technology, 2015)

Xiu, Matt, BluePath Labs, personal correspondence, 28 August-29 December 2020

Yang, Fangqing; Wang, Chao; Liao, Quanmi; and Huang, Sheng, 'A simulative method for evaluating the resistance of the flight deck's operational capability to the attack of anti-ship weapons', *International Journal of Naval Architecture and Ocean Engineering* 8 (2016), pp.563–576

Zhao, Tong, Senior Fellow, Carnegie-Tsinghua Center for Global Policy, Beijing, interview by author, Singapore, 12 February 2021

Secondary Sources

Acton, James M., *Silver Bullet? Asking the Right Questions About Conventional Prompt Global Strike* (Washington, D.C., Carnegie Endowment for Peace, 2013)

Acton, James M., *Why is Nuclear Entanglement So Dangerous?* (Carnegie Endowment for International Peace, 23 January 2019)

Acton, James M. (editor), *Russian and Chinese perspectives on non-nuclear weapons and nuclear risks* (Carnegie Endowment for International Peace, 2017), pp.9–10

Air Force Space Command, *Space Based Infrared System* (United States Air Force, last modified July 2019), <https://www.afspc.af.mil/About-Us/Fact-Sheets/Display/Article/1012596/space-based-infrared-system/>, accessed July 2020

Annual Report to Congress: Military and Security Developments Involving the People's Republic of China 2020, Office of the Secretary of Defense, https://media.defense.gov/2020/Sep/01/2002488689/-1/-1/1/2020-DOD-CHINA-MILITARY-POWER-REPORT-FINAL.PDF

Asia-Pacific Regional Security Assessment 2017, International Institute for Strategic Studies (London: IISS, 2017)

Boyd, Henry, *2019 Pentagon report: China's Rocket Force trajectory* (International Institute for Strategic Studies, 2019)

Cheek, Timothy, The Chinese People Have Stood Up September 1949, in: *Mao Zedong and China's Revolutions*, The Bedford Series in History and Culture (New York: Palgrave Macmillan, 2002)

China Power Team, 'Does China Have an Effective Sea-based Nuclear Deterrent?', *China Power* (28 December 2015, updated

26 August 2020), <https://chinapower.csis.org/ssbn/>, accessed 14 January 2021

China's National Defense in the New Era, Xinhua (2019), <http://www.xinhuanet.com/english/2019-07/24/c_138253389.htm>, accessed 27 March 2021

Clark, Bryan, *Commanding the Seas: A Plan to Reinvigorate U.S. Navy Surface Warfare* (Washington, D.C., Center for Strategic and Budgetary Assessments, 2014), p.17.

Clark, Bryan, Adam Lemon, Peter Haynes, Kyle Libby, Gillian Evans, *Regaining the High Ground at Sea: Transforming the U.S. Navy's Carrier Air Wing for Great Power Competition*, Center for Strategic and Budgetary Assessments (2018), https://csbaonline.org/research/publications/regaining-the-high-ground-at-sea-transforming-the-u.s.-navys-carrier-air-wi/publication/1, accessed 6 March 2021

Colby, Elbridge A., Testimony Before the Senate Armed Services Committee Hearing on Implementation of the National Defense Strategy, January 29, 2019, <https://www.armed-services.senate.gov/imo/media/doc/Colby_01-29-19.pdf>, accessed 7 March 2021

Cole, Bernard D., *Asian Maritime Strategies: Navigating Troubled Waters* (Annapolis: Naval Institute Press, 2013)

Congressional Research Service, *Conventional Prompt Global Strike and Long-Range Ballistic Missiles: Background and Issues* (Washington, D.C., 2020)

Congressional Research Service, *Navy Lasers, Railgun, and Gun-Launched Guided Projectile: Background and Issues for Congress* (Washington, D.C., 2020)

Dahm, J. Michael, *Air and Surface Radar* (Johns Hopkins Applied Physics Laboratory, 2020), pp.10–12

Defense Intelligence Ballistic Missile Analysis Committee, Ballistic and Cruise Missile Threat, June 2017, <https://www.nasic.af.mil/LinkClick.aspx?fileticket=F2VLcKSmCTE%3d&portalid=19>, accessed 4 March 2021

Department of Defense, Office of the Director of Testing and Evaluation, *FY 2011 Annual Report* (Washington, D.C., Department of Defense, 2011)

Demidovich, Nickolas, *Launch Vehicle Failure Mode Database* (Federal Aviation Administration, 2007)

Dunnigan, James F. and Albert A. Nofi, *Victory at Sea: World War II in the Pacific* (New York: William Morrow, 1995), pp.164–165

Erickson, Andrew S., 'Testimony before hearing on China's advanced weapons' U.S.-China Economic and Security Review Commission (2017), < https://www.andrewerickson.com/2017/02/my-testimony-before-the-u-s-china-commission-chinese-anti-ship-ballistic-missile-development-and-counter-intervention-efforts-hearing-on-chinas-advanced-wea/> accessed December 2020

Erickson, Andrew S., *Chinese Anti-Ship Ballistic Missile Development: Drivers, Trajectories and Strategic Implications* (Washington, D.C.; The Jamestown Foundation, 2013), p.64

Federation of American Scientists, *Appearance of Apparent Antiship Missile Targets in Gobi Test Areas in 2013* (Federation of American Scientists, 15 September 2014)

Federation of American Scientists, 'DDG-51 ARLEIGH BURKE-class' *FAS Military Analysis Network* (last updated 2 November 2016), <https://fas.org/man/dod-101/sys/ship/ddg-51.htm>, accessed January 2021

Fox, Charles L., 'How much is not enough? The non-nuclear Air Battle in NATO's Central', Naval War College Review 33, no. 2 (March-April 1980), <https://digital-commons.usnwc.edu/cgi/viewcontent. cgi?article=5279&context=nwc-review>

Fravel, Taylor, 'The Evolution of China's Military Strategy: Comparing the 1987 and 1999 Editions of *Zhanlüexue*', in James Mulvenon and David Finkelstein (eds.) *China's Revolution in Doctrinal Affairs: Emerging Trends in the Operational Art of the Chinese People's Liberation Army*, <http://web.mit.edu/fravel/www/fravel.2005.evolution.china.military.strategy.pdf>, accessed 27 March 2021

Gerson, Michael S., 'The Sino-Soviet Border Conflict: Deterrence, Escalation, and the Threat of Nuclear War in 1969', Center for Naval Analyses (2010), <https://www.cna.org/cna_files/pdf/d0022974.a2.pdf>, accessed 7 March 2021

Glaser, Bonnie S.; Funaiole, Matthew P.; and Hart, Brian, 'Breaking Down China's 2020 Defense Budget', *Center for Strategic and International Studies* (22 May 2020), <https://www.csis.org/analysis/breaking-down-chinas-2020-defense-budget>, accessed 14 January 2021

Heginbotham, Eric, et al, *The US-China Military Scorecard: Forces, Geography and the Evolving Balance of Power 1996-2017* (Santa Monica, CA; RAND Corporation, 2017)

Hendrix, Henry J., *To Provide and Maintain a Navy: Why Naval Primacy is America's First Best Strategy* (Annapolis: Focsle LLP, 2020)

International Institute for Strategic Studies, *China's Cyber Power in a New Era*, https://www.iiss.org/publications/strategic-dossiers/asiapacific-regional-security-assessment-2019/rsa19-07-chapter-5

Kristensen, Hans M. & Norris Robert S., *North Korean Nuclear Capabilities* (Bulletin of the Atomic Scientists, 2018)

Mao Zedong, *Mao on Warfare*, Arthur Waldron (ed.) (New York: CN Times Books, Inc, 2013)

Missile Threat, 'MGM-31B Pershing 2', *CSIS Missile Defense Project* (15 February 2017), <https://missilethreat.csis.org/missile/mgm-31b-pershing-2/>, accessed 19 January 2021

Missile Threat, 'DF-21 (Dong Feng-21/CSS-5)', *CSIS Missile Defense Project* (2020), <https://missilethreat.csis.org/missile/df-21/>, accessed December 2020

Missile Threat, 'DF-26 (Dong Feng-26)', *CSIS Missile Defense Project* (8 January 2018, last modified 23 June 2020), <https://missilethreat.csis.org/missile/dong-feng-26-df-26/>, accessed January 2021

Missile Threat, 'Standard Missile 3', *CSIS Missile Defense Project* (2020), < https://missilethreat.csis.org/defsys/sm-3/>, accessed 18 July 2020

Missile Threat, 'Standard Missile-6 (SM-6)', *CSIS Missile Defense Project* (14 April 2016, last modified 15 June 2018), <https://missilethreat.csis.org/defsys/sm-6/>, accessed 11 February 2021

Missile Threat, 'DF-15 (Dong Feng-15 / M-9 / CSS-6)', *CSIS Missile Defense Project* (11 January 2017, last modified 6 January 2020), <https://missilethreat.csis.org/missile/df-15-css-6/>, accessed 2 April 2020

Missile Threat, 'SS-N-6 / R-27', Missile Threat, *CSIS Missile Defense Project* (16 May 2017, last modified 15 June 2018), <https://missilethreat.csis.org/missile/ss-n-6-r-27-serb/>, accessed 4 June 2020

MODULE 2—CARRIER BATTLEGROUP & Amphibious Ready Group (ARG) PLATFORMS AND MISSIONS, Ready-for-Sea Handbook United States Naval Reserve Intelligence Program, <https://fas.org/irp/doddir/navy/rfs/part02.htm>, accessed 27 March, 2021

Naval History and Heritage Command, Birmingham I (Scout Cruiser No. 2), https://www.history.navy.mil/research/histories/ship-histories/danfs/b/birmingham-i.html, accessed 27 March 2021

Nuclear Threat Initiative, 'China Hexi Chemical and Machinery Corporation', NTI (2012), <https://www.nti.org/learn/facilities/10/> accessed 15 January 2021

Office of the Secretary of Defense, *Military and Security Developments Involving the People's Republic of China* (Washington, D.C., Office of the Secretary of Defense, 2020)

Pickering, Thomas, U.S. Under Secretary of State, Oral Presentation to the Chinese Government Regarding the Accidental Bombing of the PRC Embassy in Belgrade, US Department of State (1999), https://1997-2001.state.gov/policy_remarks/1999/990617_pickering_emb.html>, accessed 7 March 2021

Pilger, Michael, *China's New YJ-18 Antiship Cruise Missile: Capabilities and Implications for U.S. Forces in the Western Pacific* (Washington, D.C.; U.S.-China Economic and Security Review Commission, 28 October 2015), pp.2–3

Schulte, John C., *An Analysis of the Historical Effectiveness of Antiship Cruise Missiles in Littoral Warfare* (Monterey, CA, Naval Postgraduate School, 2004), p.x

Schwartz, Paul N., *U.S. Navy Deploying New Measures to Counter Russian Cruise Missile Threat* (Center for Strategic and International Studies, March 2015)

Scobell, Andrew and Larry Wortzel (eds.), 'Civil-Military Change in China: Elites, Institutes, and Ideas After the 16th Party Congress', *Strategic Studies Institute*, US Army War College (2004), p.6, <https://www.mitre.org/sites/default/files/publications/bruzdzinski_demystify.pdf>, accessed 7 March 2021

Scobell, Andrew, Michael McMahon, and Cortez A. Cooper III, China's Aircraft Carrier Program: Drivers, Developments, Implications, *Naval War College Review*, 68/4 (2015), <https://digital-commons.usnwc.edu/nwc-review/vol68/iss4/7>

Shugart, Cdr. Thomas, 'First Strike: China's Missile Threat to US Bases in Asia', Center for New American Security (2017), <https://www.cnas.org/publications/reports/first-strike-chinas-missile-threat-to-u-s-bases-to-asia>, accessed 4 March 2021

Stokes, Mark; Alvarado, Gabriel; Weinstein, Emily; and Easton, Ian, *China's Space and Counterspace Capabilities and Activities* (The U.S.-China Economic and Security Review Commission, 2020)

Stumpf, David K., *Reentry Vehicle Development Leading to the Minuteman Avco Mark V and 11* (Air Power History, 2017)

Tellis, Ashley J., 'India's ASAT Test: An Incomplete Success', *Carnegie Endowment for International Peace* (15 April 2019), <https://carnegieendowment.org/2019/04/15/india-s-asat-test-incomplete-success-pub-78884>, accessed 1 May 2020

Tkacik, John, 'China: Wealthy State, Strong Army -- and a Powerful Party', Heritage Foundation (2008), https://www.heritage.org/asia/report/china-wealthy-state-strong-army-and-powerful-party, accessed 27 March 2021

Union of Concerned Scientists, *Whose Finger is On the Button?* (Union of Concerned Scientists, 22 September 2017)

U.S. Department of Defense, *Cyber Strategy Summary 2018* (Washington, D.C., 2018)

U.S. Department of Defense, *DOD Dictionary of Military and Associated Terms* (2021), <https://www.jcs.mil/Portals/36/Documents/Doctrine/pubs/dictionary.pdf>

Williams, Ian and Masao Dahlgren, 'More than Missiles: China Previews its New Way of War' (2019) Center for Strategic & International Studies, <https://www.csis.org/analysis/more-missiles-china-previews-its-new-way-war>, accessed 4 March 2021

Yao Yunzhu, The Evolution of Military Doctrine of the Chinese PLA from 1985 to 1995, *Korean Journal of Defense Analysis* 7/2 (1995), https://doi.org/10.1080/10163279509464316, accessed 27 March 2021

Yengst, William, *Lightning Bolts: First Maneuvering Reentry Vehicles* (Mustang, OK; Tate Publishing & Enterprises, 2010)

Yoshihara, Toshi, Chinese Missile Strategy and the US Naval Presence in Japan, Naval War College Review 63 3/4, <https://digital-commons.usnwc.edu/nwc-review/vol63/iss3/4/>, accessed 4 March 2021

Zhao Lijian, PRC Foreign Ministry Spokesperson, Regular Press Conference January 15, 2021, Ministry of Foreign Affairs of the People's Republic of China, <https://www.fmprc.gov.cn/mfa_eng/xwfw_665399/s2510_665401/t1846677.shtml>, accessed 7 March 2021

Zhao, Tong, *The Survivability of China's SSBNs and Strategic Stability* (Beijing, Carnegie-Tsinghua Center for Global Policy, 2018)

Zheng Wang, National Humiliation, History Education, and the Politics of Historical Memory: Patriotic Education Campaign in China, *International Studies Quarterly* 52:4 (2008), https://doi.org/10.1111/j.1468-2478.2008.00526.x

Articles

ANI news service, 'China's eye in the sky: An Analysis of China's satellite surveillance', *Asia News International* (30 October 2019), <https://www.aninews.in/news/world/asia/chinas-eye-in-the-sky-an-analysis-of-chinas-satellite-surveillance20191030080635/>, accessed January 2021

Axe, David, 'The 1 Reason Navy Aircraft Carriers Could Lose a Battle to Russia or China', The National Interest (2018), https://nationalinterest.org/blog/buzz/1-reason-navy-aircraft-carriers-could-lose-battle-russia-or-china-38912, accessed 27 March 2021

Barno, David and Nora Bensahel, 'A New Generation of Unrestricted Warfare', War on the Rocks (2016), <https://warontherocks.com/2016/04/a-new-generation-of-unrestricted-warfare/>, accessed 27 March 2021

BBC News, 'China building 'great wall of sand' in South China Sea', April 1, 2015, https://www.bbc.com/news/world-asia-32126840, accessed 27 March 2021

Black, Norman, 'How to Make an Aircraft Carrier Vanish', *The Associated Press* (8 August 1986), <https://apnews.com/article/498fce4717dfd3be940a0cd8630c9f12>, accessed 21 January 2021

Blanchard, Ben, 'China holds massive military parade, to cut troop levels by 300,000', *Thomson Reuters* (3 September 2015), <https://www.reuters.com/article/us-ww2-anniversary-china-xi/china-holds-massive-military-parade-to-cut-troop-levels-by-300000-idUSKCN0R305P20150903>, accessed 18 April 2020

Bowman, Tom, Farewell: USS Enterprise Starred in History and Film, NPR, <https://www.npr.org/2012/12/01/166242595/farewell-uss-enterprise>

Broad, William J.; and Sanger, David E., *China Tests Anti-Satellite Weapon, Unnerving U.S.* (New York, NY, The New York Times, 2007)

Cabestan, Jean-Pierre, 'China's Djibouti Naval Base Increasing Its Power', East Asia Forum (2020), <https://www.eastasiaforum.org/2020/05/16/chinas-djibouti-naval-base-increasing-its-power/>, accessed 6 March 2021

Carter, James, 'How Close, Exactly, Were Russia and China to Nuclear War?', SupChina (2021), <https://supchina.com/2021/03/03/how-close-exactly-were-russia-and-china-to-nuclear-war/>, accessed 7 March 2021

Chan, Minnie, 'Chinese Military: Fourth Aircraft Carrier Likely to Be Nuclear Powered, Sources Say', South China Morning Post (13 March 2021), <https://www.scmp.com/news/china/diplomacy/article/3125224/chinese-military-fourth-aircraft-carrier-likely-be-nuclear>, accessed 27 March 2021

Chan, Minnie, 'South China Sea: Chinese Military Deploys Ballistic Missile's Launchers for Training', South China Morning Post (2021), <https://www.scmp.com/news/china/military/article/3119203/south-china-sea-chinese-military-deploys-ballistic-missiles>, accessed 4 March 2021

Chen Heying, 'New missiles meant for defensive purposes', Global Times (4 September 2015), <https://www.globaltimes.cn/content/940518.shtml>, accessed 20 December 2020

Clover, Charles, 'China Parades 'Carrier-Killer' Missile Through Beijing', Financial Times (2015), <https://www.ft.com/content/b94d907a-507a-11e5-b029-b9d50a74fd14>, accessed 8 March, 2021

Dujardin, Peter, 'USS America's Sunken Location Revealed', Newport News Daily Press (20 November 2006), <https://www.dailypress.com/news/dp-xpm-20061120-2006-11-20-0611200037-story.html>, accessed 20 December 2020

Eckstein, Megan, 'SECNAV Braithwaite Calls for New U.S. 1st Fleet Near Indian, Pacific Oceans', USNI News (17 November 2020), <https://news.usni.org/2020/11/17/secnav-braithwaite-calls-for-new-u-s-1st-fleet-near-indian-pacific-oceans>, accessed 17 December 2020

Erickson, Andrew S., 'China's DF-21D And DF-26B ASBMs: Is America Ready?', 1945 (15 November 2020), <https://www.19fortyfive.com/2020/11/chinas-df-21d-and-df-26b-asbms-is-the-u-s-military-ready/>, accessed 11 February 2021

Fravel, Taylor, 'Revising Deng's Foreign Policy', The Diplomat (2012), <https://thediplomat.com/2012/01/revising-dengs-foreign-policy-2/>, accessed 27 March 2021

Fung, Brian, 'Shootering Is the New Eastwooding: China's Aircraft Carrier Gets a Meme' (The Atlantic, Nov. 29, 2012), <https://www.theatlantic.com/international/archive/2012/11/shootering-is-the-new-eastwooding-chinas-aircraft-carrier-gets-a-meme/265678/>

Gady, Franz-Stefan, 'China Tests New Weapon Capable of Breaching US Missile Defense Systems', The Diplomat (2016), <https://thediplomat.com/2016/04/china-tests-new-weapon-capable-of-breaching-u-s-missile-defense-systems/>, accessed 4 March 2021

Garamone, Jim, 'Missile Defense Becomes Part of Great Power Competition', DOD News (28 July 2020), <https://www.defense.gov/Explore/News/Article/Article/2291331/missile-defense-becomes-part-of-great-power-competition/>, accessed October 2020

Garamone, Jim, Esper Describes DOD's Increased Cyber Offensive Strategy (Washington, D.C., Defense.gov, 2019), <https://www.defense.gov/Explore/News/Article/Article/1966758/esper-describes-dods-increased-cyber-offensive-strategy/>, accessed December 2020

Gill, Bates and Ni, Adam, The People's Liberation Army Rocket Force: Reshaping China's Approach to Strategic Deterrence (Australian Institute of International Affairs, 15 September 2019)

Glenshaw, Paul, 'The First Space Ace' (Washington, D.C., Air and Space Smithsonian, April 2018)

Global Times editorial staff, 'Encircling China is Arduous and Thankless For the US: Global Times Editorial', <https://www.globaltimes.cn/page/202012/1209247.shtml>, accessed 7 March 2021

Global Times editorial staff, 'Hopefully, "carrier killer" missiles would never be used in the South China Sea', Global Times (28 August 2020), <https://www.globaltimes.cn/content/1199208.shtml>, accessed 28 January 2021

Grossman, Elaine M., 'New Details Emerge About U.S. Nuclear Missile Test Failure', Nuclear Threat Initiative (22 August 2011), <https://www.nti.org/gsn/article/new-details-emerge-about-us-nuclear-missile-test-failure/>, accessed December 2020

Harper, Jon, 'Eagle vs. Dragon: How the U.S. and Chinese Navies Stack up', National Defense Magazine (9 March 2020), <https://www.nationaldefensemagazine.org/articles/2020/3/9/eagle-vs-dragon-how-the-us-and-chinese-navies-stack-up>, accessed November 2020

Huang, Kristin, 'China's 'aircraft-carrier killer' missiles successfully hit target ship in South China Sea, PLA insider reveals', South China Morning Post (14 November 2020), <https://www.scmp.com/news/china/military/article/3109809/chinas-aircraft-carrier-killer-missiles-successfully-hit-target>, accessed 19 December 2020

Huang, Kristin, China's new KJ-600 surveillance aircraft completes latest test flight (South China Morning Post, 28 January 2021)

Joe, Rick, 'China's Growing High-End Military Drone Force', The Diplomat (27 November 2019), <https://thediplomat.com/2019/11/chinas-growing-high-end-military-drone-force/>, accessed January 2021

Keller, John, 'The emerging China hypersonic weapons threat to surface vessels at sea', Military and Aerospace Electronics (2019), <https://www.militaryaerospace.com/unmanned/article/16711522/the-emerging-china-hypersonic-weapons-threat-to-surface-vessels-at-sea>, accessed 4 March 2021

Keller, John, Navy asks Raytheon to support ROTHR over-the-horizon surveillance radar system to monitor drug smuggling (Military & Aerospace Electronics, 18 July 2019)

Kreisher, Otto, China's Carrier Killer: Threat and Theatrics (Air Force Magazine, December 2013), p.46

Kube, Courtney; Johnson, Alex; Jackson Hallie; and Smith, Alexander, 'U.S. Launches Missiles at Syrian Base Over Chemical Weapons Attack', NBC News (7 April 2017), <https://www.nbcnews.com/news/us-news/u-s-launches-missiles-syrian-base-after-chemical-weapons-attack-n743636>, accessed 15 December 2021

Kuhn, Anthony, 'China Is Placing Underwater Sensors In The Pacific Near Guam', National Public Radio (6 February 2018), <https://www.npr.org/sections/parallels/2018/02/06/582390143/china-is-placing-underwater-sensors-in-the-pacific-near-guam>, accessed 3 February 2021

Kulacki, Gregory, 'Would China Use Nuclear Weapons First in a War With the United States?', The Diplomat (27 April 2020), <https://thediplomat.com/2020/04/would-china-use-nuclear-weapons-first-in-a-war-with-the-united-states/>, accessed 12 November 2020

Lacinski, U.S. Navy Lieutenant (Junior Grade) Samuel S., 'Navy Boost Phase Intercept Could Counter North Korea', *U.S. Naval Institute Proceedings* (August 2017), <https://www.usni.org/magazines/proceedings/2017/august/navy-boost-phase-intercept-could-counter-north-korea>, accessed June 2020

LaGrone, Sam, 'Navy, Missile Defense Agency Succeed During SM-6 Ballistic Missile Defense Test', *USNI News* 30 August 2017), <https://news.usni.org/2017/08/30/video-navy-missile-defense-agency-succeed-sm-6-ballistic-missile-defense-test>, accessed 19 December 2020

LaGrone, Sam, 'USS John S. McCain Back to Sea After Completing Repairs from Fatal 2017 Collision', US Naval Institute News (2019), <https://news.usni.org/2019/10/27/uss-john-s-mccain-back-to-sea-after-completing-repairs-from-fatal-2017-collision>, accessed 4 March 2021

LaGrone, Sam, 'USS Mason Fired 3 Missiles to Defend From Yemen Cruise Missiles Attack', *USNI News* (11 October 2016), <https://news.usni.org/2016/10/11/uss-mason-fired-3-missiles-to-defend-from-yemen-cruise-missiles-attack>, accessed 3 May 2020

Larter, David B., 'US Navy looks to hire thousands more sailors as service finds itself 9,000 sailors short at sea', *Navy Times* (10 February 2020), <https://www.navytimes.com/smr/federal-budget/2020/02/11/us-navy-looks-to-hire-thousands-more-sailors-as-service-finds-itself-9000-sailors-short-at-sea/>, accessed December 2020

Levick, Ewen, 'China's "Underwater Great Wall"', *The Maritime Executive* (18 June 2018), <https://www.maritime-executive.com/editorials/china-s-underwater-great-wall>, accessed January 2021

Liu Xuanzun, 'China's ship-killer missiles mobilized to Northwest China plateau', *Global Times* (1 September 2019), <https://www.globaltimes.cn/content/1135138.shtml>, accessed November 2020

Liu Xuanzun, 'China's J-20 fighter jets show superiority over previous generation counterparts', *Global Times* (15 September 2020), <https://www.globaltimes.cn/content/1200941.shtml>, accessed 28 December 2020

Liu Xuanzun, 'PLA Rocket Force launches DF-26 'aircraft carrier killer' missile in fast-reaction drills', *Global Times* (6 August 2020), <https://www.globaltimes.cn/content/1196944.shtml>, accessed December 2020

Liu Xuanzun, 'Reported PLA anti-ship ballistic missile launches 'show saturated attack capability'', *Global Times* (27 August 2020), <https://www.globaltimes.cn/content/1199110.shtml>, accessed December 2020

Liu Zhen, 'Chinese army sends DF-26 ballistic missiles to northwest region', *South China Morning Post* (11 January 2019), < https://www.scmp.com/news/china/military/article/2181773/chinese-army-sends-df-26-ballistic-missiles-northwest-region>, accessed 18 December 2020

MacKinnon, Rebecca, Brent Sadler, Chris Black, Andrea Koppel, Chinese in Belgrade, Beijing Protest NATO Embassy Bombing, CNN (1999), <http://edition.cnn.com/WORLD/asiapcf/9905/09/china.protest.03/>, accessed 7 March 2021

Martina, Michael 'China showcases fearsome new missiles to counter U.S. at military parade', *Thomson Reuters* (1 October 2019), <https://www.reuters.com/article/us-china-anniversary-military/china-showcases-fearsome-new-missiles-to-counter-u-s-at-military-parade-idUSKBN1WG342>, accessed 14 May 2020

Minnick, Wendell, 'China's Parade Puts US Navy on Notice', Defense News (2021), <https://www.defensenews.com/naval/2015/09/03/china-s-parade-puts-us-navy-on-notice/>, accessed 4 March 2021

Mitchell, Ellen, 'Navy pulls plug on $500 million railgun effort', The Hill (2021), <https://thehill.com/policy/defense/561231-navy-pulls-plug-on-500-million-railgun-effort>, accessed 12 July 2021

Mizokami, Kyle, 'Everything We Know About the Air Force's Secret X-37B Spaceplane', *Popular Mechanics* (30 July 2019), <https://www.popularmechanics.com/military/research/a28543381/x-37b/>, accessed 17 April 2020

Nakashima, Ellen, *Trump approved cyber-strikes against Iranian computer database used to plan attacks on oil tankers* (Washington, D.C., The Washington Post, 22 June 2019)

Panda, Ankit, *'Did China Start Testing Anti-Ship Ballistic Missiles Into the South China Sea?',* The Diplomat (2 July 2019), <https://thediplomat.com/2019/07/did-china-start-testing-anti-ship-ballistic-missiles-into-the-south-china-sea/>, accessed 4 January 2021

Pandey, Air Marshal (Ret.) B.K., 'Boosting Air Defence Capability' *SP's Aviation* (2015), <http://sps-aviation.com/story/?id=1646&h=Boosting-Air-Defence-Capability>, accessed 6 February 2021

Pollack, Joshua H. and Scott LaFoy, 'China's DF-26: A Hot-Swappable Missile?', Arms Control Wonk (2020), <https://www.armscontrolwonk.com/archive/1209405/chinas-df-26-a-hot-swappable-missile/>, accessed 4 March 2021

Prine, Carl, 'Focus: How sailors save ships like the Fitzgerald', *San Diego Union-Tribune* (21 June 2017), <https://www.sandiegouniontribune.com/military/sd-me-damage-control-20170621-story.html>, accessed 20 December 2020

Raymond, Col. Jay, 'Operations Group blazes new trail during Operation Burnt Frost', *peterson.spaceforce.mil* (2008), <https://www.peterson.spaceforce.mil/News/Article/328607/operations-group-blazes-new-trail-during-operation-burnt-frost/>, accessed 12 April 2020

Reuters staff, 'U.S. warships transit Taiwan Strait, China denounces 'provocation'', Thomson Reuters (31 December 2020), <https://www.reuters.com/article/us-taiwan-security-usa-idUSKBN2942HJ>, accessed 6 January 2021

Roblin, Sebastien, Is China's DF-100 Missile Good Enough to Kill America's Navy?' (2019), <https://nationalinterest.org/blog/buzz/chinas-df-100-missile-good-enough-kill-americas-navy-96476>, accessed 4 March 2021

Ross, Angus, Rethinking the U.S. Navy's Carrier Fleet, War on the Rocks (21 Jul. 2020), <https://warontherocks.com/2020/07/rethinking-the-u-s-navys-carrier-fleet/>, accessed 26 March 2021

Shelbourne, Mallory, 'U.S. Admiral: China Can 'Keep Pouring Money' Into Anti-Ship Ballistic Missiles', *USNI News* (27 January 2021), <https://news.usni.org/2021/01/27/u-s-admiral-china-can-keep-pouring-money-into-anti-ship-ballistic-missiles>, accessed February 2021

Smith, Rebecca, and Barry, Rob, *America's Electrical Grid Has a Vulnerable Back Door—and Russia Walked Through It* (The Wall Street Journal, 10 January 2019)

Strout, Nathan, 'Missile Defense Agency picks 2 vendors for hypersonic weapon tracking sensor prototypes', *Defense News* (25 January 2021), <https://www.defensenews.com/battlefield-tech/space/2021/01/25/missile-defense-agency-picks-two-

vendors-for-hypersonic-weapon-tracking-sensor-prototypes/>, accessed 26 January 2021

Tadjdeh, Yasmin, 'HALIFAX FORUM NEWS: China's New Rockets Called Asymmetric Threat to U.S. Navy', *National Defense* (21 November 2020), <https://www.nationaldefensemagazine.org/articles/2020/11/21/halifax-forum-news-china-accelerating-rocket-force-capability>, accessed 9 February 2021

Tate, Andrew, 'More details emerge about detection capabilities of Type 055 destroyer's radar', *Janes* (13 October 2020), <https://www.janes.com/defence-news/news-detail/more-details-emerge-about-detection-capabilities-of-type-055-destroyers-radar>, accessed 28 January 2021

"Thunder and Lightning'- The War with Iraq', Naval History and Heritage Command, <https://www.history.navy.mil/research/library/online-reading-room/title-list-alphabetically/u/us-navy-in-desert-shield-desert-storm/the-war-with-iraq.html>

Trevithick, Joseph, 'The United States Smuggled a Russian-Made Pantsir Air Defense System out of Libya; Report (2021), <https://www.thedrive.com/the-war-zone/38964/the-united-states-smuggled-a-russian-made-pantsir-air-defense-system-out-of-libya-report>, accessed 4 March 2021

Ullrich, Lt. Col. Siegfried, 'Directed Energy: Transforming the Future of Warfare', *Purview* (27 December 2018), <https://purview.dodlive.mil/2018/12/27/directed-energy-transforming-the-future-of-warfare/>, accessed 6 January 2021

Williams, Daniel, Missiles Hit Chinese Embassy, Washington Post (1999), https://www.washingtonpost.com/wp-srv/inatl/longterm/balkans/stories/belgrade050899.htm>, accessed 7 March 2021

Wise, David W., 'The Navy Must Accept that the Aircraft Carrier Age is Ending', The National Interest (26 Feb. 2020), <https://nationalinterest.org/blog/buzz/navy-must-accept-aircraft-carrier-age-ending-126907>, accessed 27 March 2021

Wolverton, Mark, 'Piercing the Plasma: Ideas to Beat the Communications Blackout of Reentry', *Scientific American* (1 December 2009), <https://www.scientificamerican.com/article/piercing-the-plasma/>, accessed 4 April 2020

Yeo, Mike, 'China ramps up production of new airborne early warning aircraft', *Defense News* (5 February 2018), <https://www.defensenews.com/digital-show-dailies/singapore-airshow/2018/02/05/china-ramps-up-production-of-new-airborne-early-warning-aircraft/>, accessed 16 December 2020

Yang, Youlan and Yang Xin, Supersonic Aircraft Carrier Killer Lu Changjian-100 Pieces Appeared, China Times (2019), <https://www.chinatimes.com/realtimenews/20191001001547-260417?chdtv>, accessed 4 March 2021

Ziezulewicz, Geoff, Navy's 7th Fleet no stranger to high ops tempo', *Navy Times* (21 August 2017), <https://www.navytimes.com/news/your-navy/2017/08/21/navys-7th-fleet-no-stranger-to-high-ops-tempo/>, accessed February 2021

NOTES

Introduction

1   Missile Threat, 'DF-15 (Dong Feng-15 / M-9 / CSS-6)', *CSIS Missile Defense Project* (11 January 2017, last modified 6 January 2020), https://missilethreat.csis.org/missile/df-15-css-6/, accessed 2 April 2020

2   Federation of American Scientists, *Appearance of Apparent Antiship Missile Targets in Gobi Test Areas in 2013* (Federation of American Scientists, 15 September 2014)

3   Ben Blanchard, 'China holds massive military parade, to cut troop levels by 300,000', *Thomson Reuters* (3 September 2015), <https://www.reuters.com/article/us-ww2-anniversary-china-xi/china-holds-massive-military-parade-to-cut-troop-levels-by-300000-idUSKCN0R305P20150903>, accessed 18 April 2020

4   Huang, Kristin, 'China's 'aircraft-carrier killer' missiles successfully hit target ship in South China Sea, PLA insider reveals', *South China Morning Post* (14 November 2020), <https://www.scmp.com/news/china/military/article/3109809/chinas-aircraft-carrier-killer-missiles-successfully-hit-target>, accessed 19 December 2020

5   Missile Threat, 'SS-N-6 / R-27,' Missile Threat, *CSIS Missile Defense Project* (16 May 2017, last modified 15 June 2018), <https://missilethreat.csis.org/missile/ss-n-6-r-27-serb/>, accessed 4 June 2020

6   Missile Threat, 'MGM-31B Pershing 2', *CSIS Missile Defense Project* (15 February 2017), https://missilethreat.csis.org/missile/mgm-31b-pershing-2/, accessed 19 January 2021

7   Raytheon, 'SM-6 Missile', *Raytheonmissilesanddefense.com* (last modified 4 April 2020), <https://www.raytheonmissilesanddefense.com/capabilities/products/sm6-missile>, accessed 6 June 2020

8   Air Force Space Command, *Space Based Infrared System* (United States Air Force, last modified July 2019), <https://www.afspc.af.mil/About-Us/Fact-Sheets/Display/Article/1012596/space-based-infrared-system/>, accessed July 2020

9   Michael Martina, 'China showcases fearsome new missiles to counter U.S. at military parade', *Thomson Reuters* (1 October 2019), < https://www.reuters.com/article/us-china-anniversary-military/china-showcases-fearsome-new-missiles-to-counter-u-s-at-military-parade-idUSKBN1WG342>, accessed 14 May 2020

Chapter 1

1   Birmingham I (Scout Cruiser No. 2), Naval History and Heritage Command, <https://www.history.navy.mil/research/histories/ship-histories/danfs/b/birmingham-i.html>, accessed 26 March 2021

2   Birmingham I, Naval History and Heritage Command.

3   James F. Dunnigan and Albert A. Nofi, *Victory at Sea: World War II in the Pacific* (New York: William Morrow, 1995), pp.164–165

4   ''Thunder and Lightning'- The War with Iraq', Naval History and Heritage Command, <https://www.history.navy.mil/research/library/online-reading-room/title-list-alphabetically/u/us-navy-in-desert-shield-desert-storm/the-war-with-iraq.html>, accessed 26 March 2021

5   Tom Bowman, Farewell: USS Enterprise Starred in History and Film, NPR, <https://www.npr.org/2012/12/01/166242595/farewell-uss-enterprise>, accessed 26 March 2021

6   Blake's dad served aboard USS *Enterprise* during Top Gun's filming, but as he was an Electrician's Mate working on the ship's nuclear reactor so was robbed of any screen time. The family still holds a grudge against Tom Cruise and Val Kilmer.

7   Brian Fung, 'Shootering Is the New Eastwooding: China's Aircraft Carrier Gets a Meme (The Atlantic, 29 November 2012), <https://www.theatlantic.com/international/archive/2012/11/shootering-is-the-new-eastwooding-chinas-aircraft-carrier-gets-a-meme/265678/>, accessed 26 March 2021

8   Angus Ross, Rethinking the U.S. Navy's Carrier Fleet, War on the Rocks (21 July 2020), <https://warontherocks.com/2020/07/rethinking-the-u-s-navys-carrier-fleet/>, accessed 26 March 2021

9   MODULE 2—CARRIER BATTLEGROUP & Amphibious Ready Group (ARG) PLATFORMS AND MISSIONS, Ready-for-Sea Handbook United States Naval Reserve Intelligence Program, <https://fas.org/irp/doddir/navy/rfs/part02.htm>, accessed 27 March 2021

10   Charles L. Fox, 'How much is not enough? The non-nuclear Air Battle in NATO's Central', Naval War College Review 33, no. 2 (March-April 1980), <https://digital-commons.usnwc.edu/cgi/viewcontent.cgi?article=5279&context=nwc-review>.

11   David W. Wise, The Navy Must Accept that the Aircraft Carrier Age is Ending, The National Interest (26 Feb. 2020), <https://nationalinterest.org/

blog/buzz/navy-must-accept-aircraft-carrier-age-ending-126907>, accessed 27 March 2021

12 Andrew Scobell, Michael McMahon, and Cortez A. Cooper III, China's Aircraft Carrier Program: Drivers, Developments, Implications, Naval War College Review, 68/4 (2015), <https://digital-commons.usnwc.edu/nwc-review/vol68/iss4/7>.

13 Minnie Chan, Chinese Military: Fourth Aircraft Carrier Likely to Be Nuclear Powered, Sources Say, South China Morning Post (13 Mar. 2021), <https://www.scmp.com/news/china/diplomacy/article/3125224/chinese-military-fourth-aircraft-carrier-likely-be-nuclear>, accessed 27 March 2021

Chapter 2

1 Andrew S. Erickson, *Chinese Anti-Ship Ballistic Missile Development: Drivers, Trajectories and Strategic Implications* (Washington, D.C.; The Jamestown Foundation, 2013), p.1

2 Charles Clover, China Parades 'Carrier-Killer' Missile Through Beijing', Financial Times (2015), <https://www.ft.com/content/b94d907a-507a-11e5-b029-b9d50a74fd14>, accessed 4 March 2021

3 Timothy Cheek, The Chinese People Have Stood Up September 1949. In: *Mao Zedong and China's Revolutions*, The Bedford Series in History and Culture (New York: Palgrave Macmillan, 2002), p.125

4 Yao Yunzhu, The Evolution of Military Doctrine of the Chinese PLA from 1985 to 1995, *Korean Journal of Defense Analysis* 7/2 (1995), https://doi.org/10.1080/10163279509464316, accessed 27 March 2021

5 Daniel Williams, Missiles Hit Chinese Embassy, Washington Post (1999), https://www.washingtonpost.com/wp-srv/inatl/longterm/balkans/stories/belgrade050899.htm>, accessed 7 March 2021

6 Thomas Pickering, Under Secretary of State, Oral Presentation to the Chinese Government Regarding the Accidental Bombing of the PRC Embassy in Belgrade, US Department of State (1999), https://1997-2001.state.gov/policy_remarks/1999/990617_pickering_emb.html>, accessed 7 March 2021

7 Rebecca MacKinnon, Brent Sadler, Chris Black, Andrea Koppel, Chinese in Belgrade, Beijing Protest NATO Embassy Bombing, CNN (1999), <http://edition.cnn.com/WORLD/asiapcf/9905/09/china.protest.03/>, accessed 7 March 2021

8 Erickson, *Chinese Anti-Ship Ballistic Missile Development*, pp.34–36

9 Andrew Scobell and Larry Wortzel (eds.), Civil-Military Change in China: Elites, Institutes, and Ideas After the 16th Party Congress, Strategic Studies Institute, US Army War College (2004), p.6 <https://www.mitre.org/sites/default/files/publications/bruzdzinski_demystify.pdf>, accessed 7 March 2021

10 Scobell and Wortzel, 'Civil-Military Change in China', p.324

11 Mao Zedong, Mao on Warfare, Arthur Waldron (ed.) (New York: CN Times Books, Inc, 2013), p.33

12 Zheng Wang, National Humiliation, History Education, and the Politics of Historical Memory: Patriotic Education Campaign in China, *International Studies Quarterly* 52:4 (2008), https://doi.org/10.1111/j.1468-2478.2008.00526.x.

13 James Carter, 'How Close, Exactly, Were Russia and China to Nuclear War?', SupChina (2021), <https://supchina.com/2021/03/03/how-close-exactly-were-russia-and-china-to-nuclear-war/>, accessed 7 March 2021

14 Michael S. Gerson, 'The Sino-Soviet Border Conflict: Deterrence, Escalation, and the Threat of Nuclear War in 1969', Center for Naval Analyses (2010), <https://www.cna.org/cna_files/pdf/d0022974.a2.pdf>, accessed 7 March 2021

15 Full Text: China's National Defense in the New Era, Xinhua (2019), <http://www.xinhuanet.com/english/2019-07/24/c_138253389.htm>, accessed 27 March 2021

16 US Department of Defense, DOD Dictionary of Military and Associated Terms (2021), <https://www.jcs.mil/Portals/36/Documents/Doctrine/pubs/dictionary.pdf>, accessed 7 March 2021

17 Global Times editorial staff, 'Hopefully, 'Carrier Killer' Missiles Would Never Be Used in The South China Sea: Global Times Editorial', Global Times (2020), <https://www.globaltimes.cn/content/1199208.shtml>, accessed 27 March 2021

18 Bernard D. Cole, *Asian Maritime Strategies: Navigating Troubled Waters* (Annapolis: Naval Institute Press, 2013), p.106

19 Cole, Asian Maritime Strategies, p.106

20 Mao Zedong, Mao on Warfare, Arthur Waldron (ed.) (New York: CN Times Books, Inc, 2013), p.34

21 PRC Foreign Ministry Spokesperson Zhao Lijian, Regular Press Conference January 15, 2021, Ministry of Foreign Affairs of the People's Republic of China, <https://www.fmprc.gov.cn/mfa_eng/xwfw_665399/s2510_665401/t1846677.shtml>, accessed 7 March 2021

22 Global Times editorial staff, 'Encircling China is Arduous and Thankless For the US: Global Times Editorial', <https://www.globaltimes.cn/page/202012/1209247.shtml>, accessed 7 March 2021

23 Charles Clover, 'China Parades 'Carrier-Killer' Missile Through Beijing', Financial Times (2015), <https://www.ft.com/content/b94d907a-507a-11e5-b029-b9d50a74fd14>, accessed 8 March 2021

24 Elbridge A. Colby, Testimony Before the Senate Armed Services Committee Hearing on Implementation of the National Defense Strategy, January 29, 2019, <https://www.armed-services.senate.gov/imo/media/doc/Colby_01-29-19.pdf>, accessed 7 March 2021

25 Cole, Asian Maritime Strategies, p.102

26 Kristin Huang, 'China's 'Aircraft-Carrier Killer' Missiles Successfully Hit Target Ship in South China Sea, PLA Insider Reveals', South China Morning Post (2020), <https://www.scmp.com/news/china/military/article/3109809/chinas-aircraft-carrier-killer-missiles-successfully-hit-target>, accessed 27 March 2021

27 David Barno and Nora Bensahel, 'A New Generation of Unrestricted Warfare', War on the Rocks (2016), <https://warontherocks.com/2016/04/a-new-generation-of-unrestricted-warfare/>, accessed 27 March 2021

28 Taylor Fravel, 'The Evolution of China's Military Strategy: Comparing the 1987 and 1999 Editions of *Zhanlüexue*', in James Mulvenon and David Finkelstein (eds.) China's Revolution in Doctrinal Affairs: Emerging Trends in the Operational Art of the Chinese People's Liberation Army, <http://web.mit.edu/fravel/www/fravel.2005.evolution.china.military.strategy.pdf>, accessed 27 March 2021

29 *Asia-Pacific Regional Security Assessment 2017*, International Institute for Strategic Studies (IISS), London: UK, 2017, p.41

30 *Asia-Pacific Regional Security Assessment 2017* IISS, p.42

31 Liu Xuanzun,' PLA Rocket Force launches DF-26 'aircraft carrier killer' missile in fast-reaction drills', Global Times (2020), <https://www.globaltimes.cn/content/1196944.shtml>, accessed 7 March 2021

32 Global Times op-ed, Hopefully, 'Carrier Killer' Missiles Would Never Be Used in The South China Sea (2020), <https://www.globaltimes.cn/content/1199208.shtml>, accessed 7 March 2021

33 Full Text: China's National Defense in the New Era, Xinhua (2019), <http://www.xinhuanet.com/english/2019-07/24/c_138253389.htm>, accessed 27 March 2021

34 Henry J. Hendrix, *To Provide and Maintain a Navy: Why Naval Primacy is America's First Best Strategy* (Annapolis: Focsle LLP, 2020), p.72

35 Taylor Fravel, 'Revising Deng's Foreign Policy', The Diplomat (2012), <https://thediplomat.com/2012/01/revising-dengs-foreign-policy-2/>, accessed 27 March 2021

36 John Tkacik, 'China: Wealthy State, Strong Army -- and a Powerful Party', Heritage Foundation (2008), https://www.heritage.org/asia/report/china-wealthy-state-strong-army-and-powerful-party, accessed 27 March 2021

Chapter 3

1 Eric Heginbotham et al, *The US-China Military Scorecard: Forces, Geography and the Evolving Balance of Power 1996-2017* (Santa Monica, CA; RAND Corporation, 2017), p.47

2 Jeffrey Lewis, Director, East Asia Nonproliferation Project, interview by author, Singapore, 5 January 2021

3 Hans M. Kristensen & Robert S. Norris, *North Korean Nuclear Capabilities* (Bulletin of the Atomic Scientists, 2018), p.42

4 Nuclear Threat Initiative, 'China Hexi Chemical and Machinery Corporation', NTI (2012), <https://www.nti.org/learn/facilities/10/> accessed 15 January 2021

5 Missile Threat, 'DF-21 (Dong Feng-21/CSS-5)', CSIS Missile Defense Project (2020), https://missilethreat.csis.org/missile/df-21/, accessed December 2020

6 Office of the Secretary of Defense, *Military and Security Developments Involving the People's Republic of China* (Washington, D.C., Office of the Secretary of Defense, 2020), p.59

7 Andrew S. Erickson, 'Testimony before hearing on China's advanced weapons' U.S.-China Economic and Security Review Commission (2017), < https://www.andrewerickson.com/2017/02/my-testimony-before-the-u-s-china-commission-chinese-anti-ship-ballistic-missile-development-and-counter-intervention-efforts-hearing-on-chinas-advanced-wea/> accessed December 2020

8 Andrew S. Erickson, 'Testimony before hearing on China's advanced weapons' U.S.-China Economic and Security Review Commission (2017), < https://www.andrewerickson.com/2017/02/my-testimony-before-the-u-

s-china-commission-chinese-anti-ship-ballistic-missile-development-and-counter-intervention-efforts-hearing-on-chinas-advanced-wea/> accessed December 2020

9   Headquarters of the Department of the Army, *The Pershing II Firing Battery* (Washington, D.C., 1985), pp.1–6

10 Jeffrey Lewis, Director, East Asia Nonproliferation Project, interview by author, Singapore, 5 January 2021

11 Dmitry Stefanovich, research fellow, Center for International Security, Institute of World Economy and International Relations of the Russian Academy of Sciences, interview by author, Singapore, 4 February 2021

12 Makeyev Rocket Design Bureau, 'Rocket R-27K,' Makeyev Rocket Design Bureau, <http://www.makeyev.ru/activities/missile-systems/2/RaketaR27K/>, accessed 15 February 2021

13 David K. Stumpf, *Reentry Vehicle Development Leading to the Minuteman Avco Mark V and 11* (Air Power History, 2017), p.15

14 Bowen Bai, Yanming Liu, Xiaofang Lin, and Xiaoping Li, 'Effects of a reentry plasma sheath on the beam pointing properties of an array antenna', *AIP Advances* 8 (2018), p.1

15 Xie Yu, Pan Liang, and Yuan Tianbao, *Trajectory Planning for Reentry Maneuverability* (Changsha, China, National University of Defense Technology, 2015), p.9

16 Xie Yu, Pan Liang, and Yuan Tianbao, *Trajectory Planning for Reentry Maneuverability* (Changsha, China, National University of Defense Technology, 2015), p.14

17 Dmitry Stefanovich, research fellow, Center for International Security, Institute of World Economy and International Relations of the Russian Academy of Sciences, interview by author, Singapore February 4, 2021

18 Chen Heying, 'New missiles meant for defensive purposes', *Global Times* (4 September 2015), <https://www.globaltimes.cn/content/940518.shtml>, accessed 20 December 2020

19 Peter Dujardin, 'USS America's Sunken Location Revealed', *Newport News Daily Press* (20 November 2006), <https://www.dailypress.com/news/dp-xpm-20061120-2006-11-20-0611200037-story.html>, accessed 20 December 2020

20 Carl Prine, 'Focus: How sailors save ships like the Fitzgerald', *San Diego Union-Tribune* (21 June 2017), <https://www.sandiegouniontribune.com/military/sd-me-damage-control-20170621-story.html>, accessed 20 December 2020

21 Fangqing Yang, Chao Wang, Quanmi Liao, Sheng Huang, 'A simulative method for evaluating the resistance of the flight deck's operational capability to the attack of anti-ship weapons', *International Journal of Naval Architecture and Ocean Engineering* 8 (2016), pp.563–576

22 Le-Wei Li, 'High-Frequency over-the-horizon radar and ionospheric backscatter studies in China', *Radio Science*, 33:5 (1998), pp.1445–1458

23 Eric Heginbotham et al, *The U.S.-China Military Scorecard: Forces, Geography and the Evolving Balance of Power 1996-2017* (Santa Monica, CA; RAND Corporation, 2017), pp.169–170

24 J Michael Dahm, *Air and Surface Radar* (Johns Hopkins Applied Physics Laboratory, 2020), pp.10–12

25 J Michael Dahm, *Air and Surface Radar* (Johns Hopkins Applied Physics Laboratory, 2020), p.12

26 John Keller, *Navy asks Raytheon to support ROTHR over-the-horizon surveillance radar system to monitor drug smuggling* (Military & Aerospace Electronics, 18 July 2019).

27 Andrew Tate, 'More details emerge about detection capabilities of Type 055 destroyer's radar', *Janes* (13 October 2020), <https://www.janes.com/defence-news/news-detail/more-details-emerge-about-detection-capabilities-of-type-055-destroyers-radar>, accessed 28 January 2021

28 Mike Yeo, 'China ramps up production of new airborne early warning aircraft', *Defense News* (5 February 2018), <https://www.defensenews.com/digital-show-dailies/singapore-airshow/2018/02/05/china-ramps-up-production-of-new-airborne-early-warning-aircraft/>, accessed 16 December 2020

29 Kristin Huang, *China's new KJ-600 surveillance aircraft completes latest test flight* (South China Morning Post, 28 January 2021).

30 Air Marshal B.K. Pandey (Ret.), 'Boosting Air Defence Capability' *SP's Aviation* (2015), http://sps-aviation.com/story/?id=1646&h=Boosting-Air-Defence-Capability, accessed 6 February 2021

31 Rick Joe, 'China's Growing High-End Military Drone Force', *The Diplomat* (27 November 2019), https://thediplomat.com/2019/11/chinas-growing-high-end-military-drone-force/, accessed January 2021

32 Ewen Levick, 'China's "Underwater Great Wall"', *The Maritime Executive* (18 June 2018), https://www.maritime-executive.com/editorials/china-s-underwater-great-wall, accessed January 2021

33 Junhai Luo, Ying Han, Liying Fan, 'Underwater Acoustic Target Tracking: A Review', *Sensors* (2 January 2018), pp.8–9

34 Anthony Kuhn, 'China Is Placing Underwater Sensors In The Pacific Near Guam', *National Public Radio* (6 February 2018), <https://www.npr.org/sections/parallels/2018/02/06/582390143/china-is-placing-underwater-sensors-in-the-pacific-near-guam>, accessed 3 February 2021

35 ANI news service, 'China's eye in the sky: An Analysis of China's satellite surveillance', *Asia News International* (30 October 2019), https://www.aninews.in/news/world/asia/chinas-eye-in-the-sky-an-analysis-of-chinas-satellite-surveillance20191030080635/, accessed January 2021

36 Jeffrey Lewis, Director, East Asia Nonproliferation Project, interview by author, Singapore, 5 January 2021

37 Eric Heginbotham et al, *The U.S.-China Military Scorecard: Forces, Geography and the Evolving Balance of Power 1996-2017* (Santa Monica, CA; RAND Corporation, 2017), p.162

38 Eric Heginbotham et al, *The U.S.-China Military Scorecard: Forces, Geography and the Evolving Balance of Power 1996-2017* (Santa Monica, CA; RAND Corporation, 2017), pp.169–170

39 Courtney Kube, Alex Johnson, Hallie Jackson and Alexander Smith, 'U.S. Launches Missiles at Syrian Base Over Chemical Weapons Attack', *NBC News* (7 April 2017), <https://www.nbcnews.com/news/us-news/u-s-launches-missiles-syrian-base-after-chemical-weapons-attack-n743636>, accessed 15 December 2021

40 Dmitry Stefanovich, research fellow, Center for International Security, Institute of World Economy and International Relations of the Russian Academy of Sciences, interview by author, Singapore, 4 February 2021

41 Matt Xiu, BluePath Labs, personal correspondence, 28 August-29 December 2020

42 Bates Gill and Adam Ni, *The People's Liberation Army Rocket Force: Reshaping China's Approach to Strategic Deterrence* (Australian Institute of International Affairs, 15 September 2019).

43 Oriana Skylar Mastro, Center Fellow at the Freeman Spogli Institute for International Studies, Stanford University, interview by author, Singapore, 3 February 2021

44 Tong Zhao, Senior Fellow, Carnegie-Tsinghua Center for Global Policy, Beijing, interview by author, Singapore, 12 February 2021

45 Nickolas Demidovich, *Launch Vehicle Failure Mode Database* (Federal Aviation Administration, 2007).

46 Elaine M. Grossman, 'New Details Emerge About U.S. Nuclear Missile Test Failure', Nuclear Threat Initiative (22 August 2011), <https://www.nti.org/gsn/article/new-details-emerge-about-us-nuclear-missile-test-failure/>, accessed December 2020

47 Jeffrey Lewis, Director, East Asia Nonproliferation Project, interview by author, Singapore, 5 January 2021

48 Confidential technical source, interview by author, Singapore, 1 September 2020

49 Confidential technical source, interview by author, Singapore, 1 September 2020

50 Andrew S. Erickson, *Chinese Anti-Ship Ballistic Missile Development: Drivers, Trajectories and Strategic Implications* (Washington, D.C.; The Jamestown Foundation, 2013), p.64

51 Tong Zhao, Senior Fellow, Carnegie-Tsinghua Center for Global Policy, Beijing, interview by author, Singapore, 12 February 2021

Chapter 4

1   Eric Heginbotham et al, *The U.S.-China Military Scorecard: Forces, Geography and the Evolving Balance of Power 1996-2017* (Santa Monica, CA; RAND Corporation, 2017), p.153

2   Liu Xuanzun, 'PLA Rocket Force launches DF-26 'aircraft carrier killer' missile in fast-reaction drills', *Global Times* (6 August 2020), <https://www.globaltimes.cn/content/1196944.shtml>, accessed December 2020

3   Liu Xuanzun, 'Reported PLA anti-ship ballistic missile launches 'show saturated attack capability'', *Global Times* (27 August 2020), <https://www.globaltimes.cn/content/1199110.shtml>, accessed December 2020

4   Missile Threat, 'MGM-31B Pershing 2', *CSIS Missile Defense Project* (15 February 2017), https://missilethreat.csis.org/missile/mgm-31b-pershing-2/, accessed 19 January 2021

5   James M. Acton, *Silver Bullet? Asking the Right Questions About Conventional Prompt Global Strike* (Washington, D.C., Carnegie Endowment for Peace, 2013), p.37

6   William Yengst, *Lightning Bolts: First Maneuvering Reentry Vehicles* (Mustang, OK; Tate Publishing & Enterprises, 2010), p.189

7   Jeffrey Lewis, Director, East Asia Nonproliferation Project, interview by author, Singapore, 5 January 2021

8   Dmitry Stefanovich, research fellow, Center for International Security, Institute of World Economy and International Relations of the Russian Academy of Sciences, interview by author, Singapore, 4 February 2021

9   Otto Kreisher, *China's Carrier Killer: Threat and Theatrics* (Air Force Magazine, December 2013), p.46

10 Federation of American Scientists, *Appearance of Apparent Antiship Missile Targets in Gobi Test Areas in 2013* (Federation of American Scientists, 15 September 2014)

11 Ankit Panda, '*Did China Start Testing Anti-Ship Ballistic Missiles Into the South China Sea?*', *The Diplomat* (2 July 2019), <https://thediplomat.com/2019/07/did-china-start-testing-anti-ship-ballistic-missiles-into-the-south-china-sea/>, accessed 4 January 2021

12 Yasmin Tadjdeh, 'HALIFAX FORUM NEWS: China's New Rockets Called Asymmetric Threat to U.S. Navy', *National Defense* (21 November 2020), <https://www.nationaldefensemagazine.org/articles/2020/11/21/halifax-forum-news-china-accelerating-rocket-force-capability>, accessed 9 February 2021

13 Kristin Huang, 'China's 'aircraft-carrier killer' missiles successfully hit target ship in South China Sea, PLA insider reveals', *South China Morning Post* (14 November 2020), <https://www.scmp.com/news/china/military/article/3109809/chinas-aircraft-carrier-killer-missiles-successfully-hit-target>, accessed 19 December 2020

14 Liu Xuanzun, 'China's J-20 fighter jets show superiority over previous generation counterparts', *Global Times* (15 September 2020), <https://www.globaltimes.cn/content/1200941.shtml>, accessed 28 December 2020

15 Halifax International Security Forum, *#HFX2020: Admiral Philip Davidson* [video] (Halifax International Security Forum, uploaded 20 November 2020) https://youtu.be/7q5mvRJyGrw?t=1238, accessed 17 January 2021.

16 Mallory Shelbourne, 'U.S. Admiral: China Can 'Keep Pouring Money' Into Anti-Ship Ballistic Missiles', *USNI News* (27 January 2021), <https://news.usni.org/2021/01/27/u-s-admiral-china-can-keep-pouring-money-into-anti-ship-ballistic-missiles>, accessed February 2021.

17 Tien, Yew Lun, 'China builds mockups of U.S. Navy Ships in area used for missile practice', (Thomson Reuters, Nov. 8, 2021), <https://www.reuters.com/world/china/china-builds-mockups-us-navy-ships-area-used-missile-target-practice-2021-11-08/>

18 Confidential subject matter expert, interview by author, Singapore, 8 December 2020.

19 Confidential subject matter expert, interview by author, Singapore, 8 December 2020.

20 Confidential subject matter expert, interview by author, Singapore, 8 December 2020

21 Missile Threat, 'DF-26 (Dong Feng-26)', *CSIS Missile Defense Project* (8 January 2018, last modified 23 June 2020), https://missilethreat.csis.org/missile/dong-feng-26-df-26/, accessed January 2021

22 Megan Eckstein, 'SECNAV Braithwaite Calls for New U.S. 1st Fleet Near Indian, Pacific Oceans', *USNI News* (17 November 2020), <https://news.usni.org/2020/11/17/secnav-braithwaite-calls-for-new-u-s-1st-fleet-near-indian-pacific-oceans>, accessed 17 December 2020

23 Andrew Erickson, 'China's DF-21D And DF-26B ASBMs: Is America Ready?', *1945* (15 November 2020), <https://www.19fortyfive.com/2020/11/chinas-df-21d-and-df-26b-asbms-is-the-u-s-military-ready/>, accessed 11 February 2021

24 Geoff Ziezulewicz, Navy's 7th Fleet no stranger to high ops tempo', *Navy Times* (21 August 2017), <https://www.navytimes.com/news/your-navy/2017/08/21/navys-7th-fleet-no-stranger-to-high-ops-tempo/>, accessed February 2021

25 Eric Heginbotham et al, *The U.S.-China Military Scorecard: Forces, Geography and the Evolving Balance of Power 1996-2017* (Santa Monica, CA; RAND Corporation, 2017), pp.69–70

26 James M. Acton, *Why is Nuclear Entanglement So Dangerous?* (Carnegie Endowment for International Peace, 23 January 2019).

27 Oriana Skylar Mastro, Center Fellow at the Freeman Spogli Institute for International Studies, Stanford University, interview by author, Singapore, 3 February 2021

28 Actually Mike Tyson said this.

29 Federation of American Scientists, 'DDG-51 ARLEIGH BURKE-class' *FAS Military Analysis Network* (last updated 2 November 2016), <https://fas.org/man/dod-101/sys/ship/ddg-51.htm>, accessed January 2021

30 Missile Threat, 'Standard Missile-6 (SM-6)', *CSIS Missile Defense Project* (14 April 2016, last modified 15 June 2018), https://missilethreat.csis.org/defsys/sm-6/, accessed 11 February 2021

31 Office of the Secretary of Defense, *Military and Security Developments Involving the People's Republic of China* (Washington, D.C., Office of the Secretary of Defense, 2020), p.59

32 Office of the Secretary of Defense, *Military and Security Developments Involving the People's Republic of China* (Washington, D.C., Office of the Secretary of Defense, 2020), P.165

33 Eric Heginbotham et al, *The U.S.-China Military Scorecard: Forces, Geography and the Evolving Balance of Power 1996-2017* (Santa Monica, CA; RAND Corporation, 2017), pp.186–189

34 Office of the Secretary of Defense, *Military and Security Developments Involving the People's Republic of China* (Washington, D.C., Office of the Secretary of Defense, 2020), p.59

35 Paul N. Schwartz, *U.S. Navy Deploying New Measures to Counter Russian Cruise Missile Threat* (Center for Strategic and International Studies, March 2015), p.2

36 Dmitry Stefanovich, research fellow, Center for International Security, Institute of World Economy and International Relations of the Russian Academy of Sciences, interview by author, Singapore, 4 February 2021

37 David B. Larter, 'US Navy looks to hire thousands more sailors as service finds itself 9,000 sailors short at sea', *Navy Times* (10 February 2020), <https://www.navytimes.com/smr/federal-budget/2020/02/11/us-navy-looks-to-hire-thousands-more-sailors-as-service-finds-itself-9000-sailors-short-at-sea/>, accessed 11 February 2021

38 Reuters staff, 'U.S. warships transit Taiwan Strait, China denounces 'provocation'', Thomson Reuters (31 December 2020), <https://www.reuters.com/article/us-taiwan-security-usa-idUSKBN2942HJ>, accessed 6 January 2021

39 Global Times editorial staff, 'Hopefully, 'carrier killer' missiles would never be used in the South China Sea', *Global Times* (28 August 2020), <https://www.globaltimes.cn/content/1199208.shtml>, accessed 28 January 2021

40 Confidential technical source, interview by author, Singapore, 1 September 2020

41 Norman Black, 'How to Make an Aircraft Carrier Vanish', *The Associated Press* (8 August 1986), <https://apnews.com/article/498fce4717dfd3be940a0cd8630c9f12>, accessed 21 January 2021

42 Office of the Secretary of Defense, *Military and Security Developments Involving the People's Republic of China* (Washington, D.C., Office of the Secretary of Defense, 2020), pp.63–64

43 Office of the Secretary of Defense, *Military and Security Developments Involving the People's Republic of China* (Washington, D.C., Office of the Secretary of Defense, 2020), pp.74–75

44 Eric Heginbotham et al, *The U.S.-China Military Scorecard: Forces, Geography and the Evolving Balance of Power 1996-2017* (Santa Monica, CA; RAND Corporation, 2017), pp.157–159; 164–165

45 Eric Heginbotham et al, *The U.S.-China Military Scorecard: Forces, Geography and the Evolving Balance of Power 1996-2017* (Santa Monica, CA; RAND Corporation, 2017), pp.159–164

46 Eric Heginbotham et al, *The U.S.-China Military Scorecard: Forces, Geography and the Evolving Balance of Power 1996-2017* (Santa Monica, CA; RAND Corporation, 2017), pp.159–164

47 Tong Zhao, Senior Fellow, Carnegie-Tsinghua Center for Global Policy, Beijing, interview by author, Singapore, 12 February 2021

48 Eric Heginbotham et al, *The U.S.-China Military Scorecard: Forces, Geography and the Evolving Balance of Power 1996-2017* (Santa Monica, CA; RAND Corporation, 2017), p.167

49 Eric Heginbotham et al, *The U.S.-China Military Scorecard: Forces, Geography and the Evolving Balance of Power 1996-2017* (Santa Monica, CA; RAND Corporation, 2017), p.168

50 Matt Xiu, BluePath Labs, personal correspondence, 28 August-29 December 2020

51 Tong Zhao, Senior Fellow, Carnegie-Tsinghua Center for Global Policy, Beijing, interview by author, Singapore, 12 February 2021

52 Michael Pilger, *China's New YJ-18 Antiship Cruise Missile: Capabilities and Implications for U.S. Forces in the Western Pacific* (Washington, D.C.; U.S.-China Economic and Security Review Commission, 28 October 2015), pp.2–3

53 Office of the Secretary of Defense, *Military and Security Developments Involving the People's Republic of China* (Washington, D.C., Office of the Secretary of Defense, 2020), pp.63–64

54 Mike Yeo, 'China ramps up production of new airborne early warning aircraft', Defense News (5 February 2018), < https://www.defensenews.com/digital-show-dailies/singapore-airshow/2018/02/05/china-ramps-up-production-of-new-airborne-early-warning-aircraft/>, accessed 16 December 2020

55 Eric Heginbotham et al, *The U.S.-China Military Scorecard: Forces, Geography and the Evolving Balance of Power 1996-2017* (Santa Monica, CA; RAND Corporation, 2017), p.xxvi.

56 Tong Zhao, Senior Fellow, Carnegie-Tsinghua Center for Global Policy, Beijing, interview by author, Singapore, 12 February 2021

57 Dmitry Stefanovich, research fellow, Center for International Security, Institute of World Economy and International Relations of the Russian Academy of Sciences, interview by author, Singapore, 4 February 2021

58 Henry Boyd, *2019 Pentagon report: China's Rocket Force trajectory* (International Institute for Strategic Studies, 2019).

59 China Power Team, '*Does China Have an Effective Sea-based Nuclear Deterrent?*', China Power (28 December 2015, updated 26 August 2020), <https://chinapower.csis.org/ssbn/>, accessed 14 January 2021

60 Union of Concerned Scientists, *Whose Finger is On the Button?* (Union of Concerned Scientists, 22 September 2017).

62 Oriana Skylar Mastro, Center Fellow at the Freeman Spogli Institute for International Studies, Stanford University, interview by author, Singapore, 3 February 2021

62 James M. Acton (editor), *Russian and Chinese perspectives on non-nuclear weapons and nuclear risks* (Carnegie Endowment for International Peace, 2017), pp.9–10

63 Jeffrey Lewis, Director, East Asia Nonproliferation Project, interview by author, Singapore, 5 January 2021

64 Bonnie S. Glaser, Matthew P. Funaiole and Brian Hart, 'Breaking Down China's 2020 Defense Budget', *Center for Strategic and International Studies* (22 May 2020), <https://www.csis.org/analysis/breaking-down-chinas-2020-defense-budget>, accessed 14 January 2021

65 Mark Stokes, executive director, Project 2049 Institute, personal correspondence, 12 February 2021

66 Matt Xiu, BluePath Labs, personal correspondence, 28 August-29 December 2020

Chapter 5

1 U.S. Department of Defense, *Cyber Strategy Summary 2018* (Washington, D.C., 2018), p.1

2 Jim Garamone, *Esper Describes DOD's Increased Cyber Offensive Strategy* (Washington, D.C., Defense.gov, 2019), <https://www.defense.gov/Explore/News/Article/Article/1966758/esper-describes-dods-increased-cyber-offensive-strategy/>, accessed December 2020

3 Ellen Nakashima, *Trump approved cyber-strikes against Iranian computer database used to plan attacks on oil tankers* (Washington, D.C., The Washington Post, 22 June 2019).

4 Congressional Research Service, *Conventional Prompt Global Strike and Long-Range Ballistic Missiles: Background and Issues* (Washington, D.C., 2020), p.12

5 Congressional Research Service, *Conventional Prompt Global Strike and Long-Range Ballistic Missiles: Background and Issues* (Washington, D.C., 2020), p.34

6 James M. Acton, *Silver Bullet? Asking the Right Questions About Conventional Prompt Global Strike* (Washington, D.C., Carnegie Endowment for Peace, 2013), p.112

7 Tong Zhao, Senior Fellow, Carnegie-Tsinghua Center for Global Policy, Beijing, interview with author, 12 February 2021

8 Scott LaFoy, personal correspondence, 4 September 2020

9 Matt Xiu, BluePath Labs, personal correspondence, 28 August-29 December 2020

10 Liu Xuanzun, 'China's ship-killer missiles mobilized to Northwest China plateau', *Global Times* (1 September 2019), <https://www.globaltimes.cn/content/1135138.shtml>, accessed November 2020

11 Liu Zhen, 'Chinese army sends DF-26 ballistic missiles to northwest region', *South China Morning Post* (11 January 2019), < https://www.scmp.com/news/china/military/article/2181773/chinese-army-sends-df-26-ballistic-missiles-northwest-region>, accessed 18 December 2020

12 Office of the Secretary of Defense, *Military and Security Developments Involving the People's Republic of China* (Washington, D.C., Office of the Secretary of Defense, 2020), p.46

13 Matt Xiu, BluePath Labs, personal correspondence, 28 August-29 December 2020

14 Jon Harper, '*Eagle vs. Dragon: How the U.S. and Chinese Navies Stack up*', *National Defense Magazine* (9 March 2020), <https://www.nationaldefensemagazine.org/articles/2020/3/9/eagle-vs-dragon-how-the-us-and-chinese-navies-stack-up>, accessed November 2020

15 Gregory Kulacki, '*Would China Use Nuclear Weapons First in a War With the United States?*', The Diplomat (27 April 2020), <https://thediplomat.com/2020/04/would-china-use-nuclear-weapons-first-in-a-war-with-the-united-states/>, accessed 12 November 2020

16 Lieutenant (Junior Grade) Samuel S. Lacinski, U.S. Navy, 'Navy Boost Phase Intercept Could Counter North Korea', *U.S. Naval Institute Proceedings* (August 2017), <https://www.usni.org/magazines/proceedings/2017/august/navy-boost-phase-intercept-could-counter-north-korea>, accessed June 2020

17 Tong Zhao, *The Survivability of China's SSBNs and Strategic Stability* (Beijing, Carnegie-Tsinghua Center for Global Policy, 2018), p.26

18 Mark Stokes, Gabriel Alvarado, Emily Weinstein, and Ian Easton, *China's Space and Counterspace Capabilities and Activities* (The U.S.-China Economic and Security Review Commission, 2020), pp.29–30

19 Mark Stokes, Gabriel Alvarado, Emily Weinstein, and Ian Easton, *China's Space and Counterspace Capabilities and Activities* (The U.S.-China Economic and Security Review Commission, 2020), pp.31–32

20 Outer Space Treaty (New York, NY, United Nations, 1966).

21 Paul Glenshaw, 'The First Space Ace' (Washington, D.C., *Air and Space Smithsonian*, April 2018).

22 Colonel Jay Raymond, 'Operations Group blazes new trail during Operation Burnt Frost', *peterson.spaceforce.mil* (2008), <https://www.peterson.spaceforce.mil/News/Article/328607/operations-group-blazes-new-trail-during-operation-burnt-frost/>, accessed 12 April 2020

23 Kyle Mizokami, 'Everything We Know About the Air Force's Secret X-37B Spaceplane', *Popular Mechanics* (30 July 2019), <https://www.popularmechanics.com/military/research/a28543381/x-37b/>, accessed 17 April 2020

24 Ashley J. Tellis, 'India's ASAT Test: An Incomplete Success', *Carnegie Endowment for International Peace* (15 April 2019), https://carnegieendowment.org/2019/04/15/india-s-asat-test-incomplete-success-pub-78884, accessed 1 May 2020

25 William J. Broad and David E. Sanger, *China Tests Anti-Satellite Weapon, Unnerving U.S.* (New York, NY, The New York Times, 2007).

26 Raytheon, 'AN/SLQ-32(V) Shipboard EW System', *Raytheonmissilesanddefense.com* (2020), <https://www.raytheon.com/capabilities/products/slq32>, accessed 24 April 2020

27 Rebecca Smith and Rob Barry, *America's Electrical Grid Has a Vulnerable Back Door—and Russia Walked Through It* (The Wall Street Journal, 10 January 2019).

28 Andrew S. Erickson, *Chinese Anti-Ship Ballistic Missile Development: Drivers, Trajectories and Strategic Implications* (Washington, D.C.; The Jamestown Foundation, 2013), p.64

29 Mark Wolverton, 'Piercing the Plasma: Ideas to Beat the Communications Blackout of Reentry', *Scientific American* (1 December 2009), <https://www.scientificamerican.com/article/piercing-the-plasma/>, accessed 4 April 2020

30 Nathan Strout, 'Missile Defense Agency picks 2 vendors for hypersonic weapon tracking sensor prototypes', *Defense News* (25 January 2021), <https://www.defensenews.com/battlefield-tech/space/2021/01/25/missile-defense-agency-picks-two-vendors-for-hypersonic-weapon-tracking-sensor-prototypes/>, accessed 26 January 2021

31 Eric Heginbotham et al, *The U.S.-China Military Scorecard: Forces, Geography and the Evolving Balance of Power 1996-2017* (Santa Monica, CA; RAND Corporation, 2017), p.166

32 Lt. Col. Siegfried Ullrich, 'Directed Energy: Transforming the Future of Warfare', *Purview* (27 December 2018), https://purview.dodlive.mil/2018/12/27/directed-energy-transforming-the-future-of-warfare/, accessed 6 January 2021

33 Eric Heginbotham et al, *The U.S.-China Military Scorecard: Forces, Geography and the Evolving Balance of Power 1996-2017* (Santa Monica, CA; RAND Corporation, 2017), p.166

34 Andrew S. Erickson, *Chinese Anti-Ship Ballistic Missile Development: Drivers, Trajectories and Strategic Implications* (Washington, D.C.; The Jamestown Foundation, 2013), p.64

35 Eric Heginbotham et al, *The U.S.-China Military Scorecard: Forces, Geography and the Evolving Balance of Power 1996-2017* (Santa Monica, CA; RAND Corporation, 2017), p.166

36 Eric Heginbotham et al, *The U.S.-China Military Scorecard: Forces, Geography and the Evolving Balance of Power 1996-2017* (Santa Monica, CA; RAND Corporation, 2017), pp.169–170

37 Eric Heginbotham et al, *The U.S.-China Military Scorecard: Forces, Geography and the Evolving Balance of Power 1996-2017* (Santa Monica, CA; RAND Corporation, 2017), pp.166–167

38 John C. Schulte, *An Analysis of the Historical Effectiveness of Antiship Cruise Missiles in Littoral Warfare* (Monterey, CA, Naval Postgraduate School, 2004), p.x.

39 Sam LaGrone, 'USS Mason Fired 3 Missiles to Defend From Yemen Cruise Missiles Attack', *USNI News* (11 October 2016), <https://news.usni. org/2016/10/11/uss-mason-fired-3-missiles-to-defend-from-yemen-cruise-missiles-attack>, accessed 3 May 2020

40 Bryan Clark, *Commanding the Seas: A Plan to Reinvigorate U.S. Navy Surface Warfare* (Washington, D.C., Center for Strategic and Budgetary Assessments, 2014), p.17

41 Jim Garamone, 'Missile Defense Becomes Part of Great Power Competition', *DOD News* (28 July 2020), <https://www.defense.gov/ Explore/News/Article/Article/2291331/missile-defense-becomes-part-of-great-power-competition/>, accessed October 2020

42 Confidential technical source, interview by author, Singapore, 1 September 2020

43 Confidential technical source, interview by author, Singapore, 1 September 2020

44 Raytheon, 'U.S. Navy's SPY-6 Family of Radars', *Raytheonmissilesanddefense. com* (2020), <https://www.raytheonmissilesanddefense.com/capabilities/ products/spy6-radars>, accessed December 2020

45 Department of Defense, Office of the Director of Testing and Evaluation, *FY 2011 Annual Report (*Washington, D.C., Department of Defense, 2011), p.297

46 Confidential technical source, interview by author, Singapore, 1 September 2020

47 Confidential technical source, interview by author, Singapore, 1 September 2020

48 Missile Threat, 'Standard Missile 3', *CSIS Missile Defense Project* (2020), < https://missilethreat.csis.org/defsys/sm-3/>, accessed 18 July 2020

49 Sam LaGrone, '*Navy, Missile Defense Agency Succeed During SM-6 Ballistic Missile Defense Test*', *USNI News* 30 August 2017), <https://news.usni. org/2017/08/30/video-navy-missile-defense-agency-succeed-sm-6-ballistic-missile-defense-test>, accessed 19 December 2020

50 Congressional Research Service, *Navy Lasers, Railgun, and Gun-Launched Guided Projectile: Background and Issues for Congress (*Washington, D.C., 2020), p.3

51 Ellen Mitchell, 'Navy pulls plug on $500 million railgun effort', The Hill (2021), <https://thehill.com/policy/defense/561231-navy-pulls-plug-on-500-million-railgun-effort>, accessed 12 July 2020

52 Dmitry Stefanovich, research fellow, Center for International Security, Institute of World Economy and International Relations of the Russian Academy of Sciences, interview with Author, 4 February 2021

Chapter 6

1 Wendell Minnick, 'China's Parade Puts US Navy on Notice', Defense News (2021), <https://www.defensenews.com/naval/2015/09/03/china-s-parade-puts-us-navy-on-notice/>, accessed 4 March 2021

2 Joshua H. Pollack and Scott LaFoy, 'China's DF-26: A Hot-Swappable Missile?', Arms Control Wonk (2020), <https://www.armscontrolwonk. com/archive/1209405/chinas-df-26-a-hot-swappable-missile/>, accessed 4 March 2021

3 Based on BlluePath Labs, October 2020

4 *Jane's Strategic Weapons 2004, 2011*; Lewis and Hua (1999), IISS, 2019; DOD Report to Congress, 2020

5 *Annual Report to Congress: Military and Security Developments involving the People's Republic of China*, Office of the Secretary of Defence, 2019; 2020

6 Defense Intelligence Ballistic Missile Analysis Committee, Ballistic and Cruise Missile Threat, June 2017, <https://www.nasic.af.mil/LinkClick. aspx?fileticket=F2VLcKSmCTE%3d&portalid=19>, accessed 4 March 2021

7 Annual Report to Congress: Military and Security Developments Involving the People's Republic of China 2020, Office of the Secretary of Defense, https://media.defense.gov/2020/Sep/01/2002488689/-1/-1/1/2020-DOD-CHINA-MILITARY-POWER-REPORT-FINAL.PDF.

8 Matt Xiu, BluePath Labs, personal correspondence, 28 August-29 December 2020

9 BBC News, 'China building 'great wall of sand' in South China Sea,' 1 April 2015, https://www.bbc.com/news/world-asia-32126840, accessed 27 March 2021

10 Minnie Chan, 'South China Sea: Chinese Military Deploys Ballistic Missile's Launchers for Training', South China Morning Post (2021), <https://www.scmp.com/news/china/military/article/3119203/south-china-sea-chinese-military-deploys-ballistic-missiles>, accessed 4 March 2021

11 Jean-Pierre Cabestan, 'China's Djibouti Naval Base Increasing Its Power', East Asia Forum (2020), <https://www.eastasiaforum.org/2020/05/16/ chinas-djibouti-naval-base-increasing-its-power/>, accessed 6 March 2021

12 David Axe, 'The 1 Reason Navy Aircraft Carriers Could Lose a Battle to Russia or China', The National Interest (2018), <https://nationalinterest. org/blog/buzz/1-reason-navy-aircraft-carriers-could-lose-battle-russia-or-china-38912>, accessed 27 March 2021

13 Bryan Clark, Adam Lemon, Peter Haynes, Kyle Libby, Gillian Evans, *Regaining the High Ground at Sea: Transforming the U.S. Navy's Carrier Air Wing for Great Power Competition*, Center for Strategic and Budgetary Assessments (2018), <https://csbaonline.org/research/publications/ regaining-the-high-ground-at-sea-transforming-the-u.s.-navys-carrier-air-wi/publication/1>, accessed 6 March 2021

14 International Institute for Strategic Studies, China's Cyber Power in a New Era, https://www.iiss.org/publications/strategic-dossiers/asiapacific-regional-security-assessment-2019/rsa19-07-chapter-5

15 Joseph Trevithick, 'The United States Smuggled a Russian-Made Pantsir Air Defense System out of Libya: Report', The Drive (2021), <https:// www.thedrive.com/the-war-zone/38964/the-united-states-smuggled-a-russian-made-pantsir-air-defense-system-out-of-libya-report>, accessed 4 March 2021

16 Matt Xiu, personal correspondence, 28 August-8 September 2020

17 Tyler Rogoway, This is the Only Photo of a US Navy Supercarrier Being Sunk (Updated 2018), The War Zone, <https://www.thedrive.com/the-war-zone/22639/this-is-the-only-photo-of-a-u-s-navy-supercarrier-being-sunk>, accessed 4 March 2021

18 John Keller, 'The emerging China hypersonic weapons threat to surface vessels at sea', Military and Aerospace Electronics (2019), <https://www. militaryaerospace.com/unmanned/article/16711522/the-emerging-china-hypersonic-weapons-threat-to-surface-vessels-at-sea>, accessed 4 March 2021

19 Franz-Stefan Gady, 'China Tests New Weapon Capable of Breaching US Missile Defense Systems', The Diplomat (2016), <https://thediplomat. com/2016/04/china-tests-new-weapon-capable-of-breaching-u-s-missile-defense-systems/>, accessed 4 March 2021

20 Sebastien Roblin, Is China's DF-100 Missile Good Enough to Kill America's Navy?' (2019), <https://nationalinterest.org/blog/buzz/chinas-df-100-missile-good-enough-kill-americas-navy-96476>, accessed 4 March 2021

21 Ian Williams and Masao Dahlgren, 'More than Missiles: China Previews its New Way of War' (2019) Center for Strategic & International Studies, <https://www.csis.org/analysis/more-missiles-china-previews-its-new-way-war>, accessed 4 March 2021

22 Yang Youlan and Yang Xin, Supersonic Aircraft Carrier Killer Lu Changjian-100 Pieces Appeared, China Times (2019), <https://www. chinatimes.com/realtimenews/20191001001547-260417?chdtv>, accessed 4 March 2021

23 Toshi Yoshihara, Chinese Missile Strategy and the US Naval Presence in Japan, Naval War College Review 63 3/4, <https://digital-commons.usnwc. edu/nwc-review/vol63/iss3/4/>, accessed 4 March 2021

24 Cdr. Thomas Shugart, 'First Strike: China's Missile Threat to US Bases in Asia', Center for New American Security (2017), <https://www.cnas.org/ publications/reports/first-strike-chinas-missile-threat-to-u-s-bases-to-asia>, accessed 4 March 2021

25 Shugart, 'First Strike'.

26 Shugart, 'First Strike'.

27 Sam LaGrone, 'USS John S. McCain Back to Sea After Completing Repairs from Fatal 2017 Collision', US Naval Institute News (2019), <https://news. usni.org/2019/10/27/uss-john-s-mccain-back-to-sea-after-completing-repairs-from-fatal-2017-collision>, accessed 4 March 2021

ABOUT THE AUTHORS

Gerry Doyle is an editor on the Global News Desk at Thomson Reuters. He has been posted overseas for 13 years, 10 of them in Asia, with a recurring focus on defense and security. A native of Kansas City, Mo., in the United States, he has degrees in journalism and philosophy from the University of Kansas. His career has taken him from the Midwest to Florida (where he was part of the 2000 general election team) to Chicago (where he interviewed Barack Obama on a street corner) to the Middle East (just in time for the Arab Spring) before landing him in East Asia (where he helped cover the Umbrella Revolution in Hong Kong and North Korea's burgeoning nuclear weapons program). His novel, *From the Depths*, was published in 2007 and was a finalist for the American Thriller Writers' Best Debut Novel award. He lives in Singapore with his wife and two children.

A third-generation sailor, **Blake Herzinger**, joined the Navy while studying political science at Brigham Young University. He first experienced Asia as an officer in the US Navy deployed to Okinawa and moved to Singapore in 2013, completing a masters degree in strategic studies while serving as a naval liaison. He became a consultant to the U.S. Navy in the Asia-Pacific after leaving active service in 2017 but remains in the U.S. Navy Reserve. He writes regularly on naval matters and the Asia Pacific, with work published in *Foreign Policy*, *Brookings*, and *War on the Rocks*, and joined the Pacific Forum as a Non-resident WSD-Handa Fellow in 2021. He lives with his wife, son, dog and cat in Singapore.